Collecting under the Radar
Tomorrow's Antiques

Collecting
under the Radar

Tomorrow's Antiques

Michael Hogben and Linda Abrams

Red Rock Press

New York   New York

Dedications

For my five wonderful children.

—M.H.

To my husband, Greg, who doesn't have a clue what antiques
I bring into the house under the radar.

—L. A.

Table of Contents

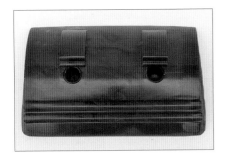
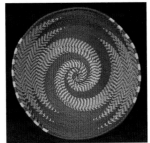

Past Pastimes

The Best of Whatever

Old Playthings

Still Looking Good

End Papers

NUT
BROWN
TOBACCO

makes an

GEE !!
I WISH I WERE
A MAN
I'd JOIN
The NAVY

Foreword

Collecting antiques has been a life-long passion for me, and the excitement and pleasure that it produces never subsides. As an art dealer for five years and an auctioneer for nearly twenty, I've had over two million lots pass through my hands at a value of some $30 million.

Some of the more fascinating collecting paths lie deep-rooted in the memory. The urge to accumulate objects from the past can lead to the formation of an immensely pleasurable collection, which can also—with a bit of luck and skill—be accompanied by considerable financial reward.

Nearly everyone has, or can develop, an eye for some nostalgic item. The urge to collect may come about in a number of random ways: all of a sudden you realize that you have just bought your third piece of art glass, or maybe you have long been gathering items connected with the area in which you grew up. Perhaps you are a fanatical gardener and have grown to admire the antique items that add such charm to that shady corner of your yard. Or maybe the implements used in kitchens past have caught your eye, especially if you are a promising chef. Chances are that an existing hobby or long-held interest is the stimulus for your collection.

Once you have made a decision as to what to collect, the field you have chosen will no doubt open up plentiful collecting possibilities, and you may have to whittle down your criteria. Should you only collect items in top condition? Should you limit yourself to the earliest examples? Perhaps only items of a certain color or size catch your eye. The choices and the fun of collecting are entirely yours, and you can be certain that you'll always feel a sense of achievement from collecting your unique assortment of items.

Although the reasons for investing in antiques are abundant—enthusiasm for or enjoyment of a particular object, or to remind yourself of days gone by—one thing is for certain: you will want your acquisitions to represent a good financial investment. Investing in antiques can be similar to investing in the stock market in that the market will always have its highs and lows. Knowing when to invest, what to invest in and how much you should pay are all crucial factors for any prospective collector.

With the lure of antiques and collecting showing no sign of slowing down, I have decided to share my over 25 years of experience with you and offer you some tips on which items I believe will be good future investments and, I hope, the subjects of enjoyable and interesting collections as well. In this book, I have chosen items which I strongly believe are destined to become the antiques of the future, meaning that they will, some time soon, become more valuable, and thus even more desirable, than they are now. (My co-author has done likewise.) Furthermore, I believe that most of the items chosen are affordable at the moment, but may not remain so in the near future.

This book includes a wide range of items, from furniture to ceramics, from jewelry to postcards, in the hope that one or more of these items will spark your interest, and will lead you to develop a passion for whatever you have chosen to collect.

It is my pleasure to share with you my "top tips" on finding, buying and maintaining each featured item so that it retains its value and integrity for as long as you own it. These are tomorrow's antiques, so get in there now, while the going's good!

Starting a collection

There are some basic rules that any collector, whether established or novice, should follow. Some of these may seem obvious, but I think they are worth mentioning lest you get caught up in the excitement of a sale and forget your common sense!

Do your research

Once you have chosen a subject to collect, one of the best investments you will make will be reference books, magazines and articles on your chosen subject. These reference materials will help you to educate yourself on what you are about to collect, and we all know how important an education is. Many libraries have an antiques and collectors reference section, so it may be an idea to pop down to your local library and borrow books until you figure out what (reference or collectible) might be worth owning. If your local branch doesn't have a book you want, it may be able to find it for you elsewhere in its library network.

You should also keep your eyes and ears open for collectors' clubs and exhibitions relating to your chosen subject. The knowledge you will attain is bound to enhance the pleasure to be gained from your own purchases. Furthermore, this is a good way to meet other collectors with common interests, and who may have items from their collections that they wish to sell—an easy way to expand your own collection! Conversely, should you decide that you wish to sell an item from your collection (perhaps because you want to realize a portion of your financial investment, or perhaps to make space for the display of a new addition to your collection), you may find that you have a buyer right under your nose!

Joining a collectors' club will also allow you to keep abreast of current trends in the area that you are collecting, which can be very useful in terms of knowing the value of what you own.

Buying and selling your collection

Antiques shows, charity fairs and even some flea markets are excellent places to visit to familiarize yourself with the antiques and memorabilia trade as a whole. When you start to know your collecting fields, you'll begin to spot bargains. Fairs with collectibles are also a great place to sell your own stuff, especially if you want to get rid of a lot of items quickly. Check community bul-

letin boards at your local school, religious or neighborhood center and supermarket for information on when and where sales are being held.

Internet

The Internet is a great place to get an idea of what an object might be worth, making it a good starting point for any collection. The famous auction site, eBay, is a fantastic place to look, as you can get a true sense of an item's value through the bidding process. You might also have a look at the websites of some of the more famous auction houses, such as Christie's and Sotheby's. You can even check their recent auctions online to see how much money an item is selling, or has sold, for. And then, of course, you can use some sites to buy and sell your own items.

Auction Houses

Depending on what you collect, you may find an auction room an excellent place to buy or sell pricier pieces. Like all businesses, auction houses have to make a profit to survive, and they do this by charging the vendor (the seller) a commission charge; the buyer is charged a buyer's premium.

Commission charges vary from a staggering 25 percent to 10 percent. Sellers' commissions sometimes can be negotiated down, especially on expensive items. Or, for instance, if you have a complete house's contents to be auctioned, chances are that the auction house will negotiate a competitive commission rate, sometimes as low as five percent. If you have many items that you wish to sell, it is almost always worth negotiating with an auction house.

Auction houses will also charge an insurance fee or percentage, and add transport and illustration charges on top of their commission. This is all negotiable, but make sure you know how much you are going to be charged before you put your goods into the auction sale.

In my opinion, it is always worth consulting two salerooms to find out where you will get the best deal on the commission rate. If you have a special item, I would recommend that you find an auction room that produces a nice glossy catalogue with illustrations.

Buyers can sometimes knock off a couple of commission points by paying cash. Whether selling or buying, you need to settle on the rules well before bidding begins.

Damage and restoration

This is a subject worth knowing a bit about, as virtually every collector of older items is bound to encounter damaged or restored examples. In fact, I think it is safe to assume that fewer than ten percent of all objects bought and sold in the vintage and antiques trades can be considered in perfect condition. Regrettably, no amount of careful handling or protection can prevent all damage; it is just a fact of life that the process of natural decay and the elements make some materials more prone to rapid deterioration than others. That said, some of the most obviously fragile man-made materials, including glass and porcelain, are, in fact, the most resilient.

Collectors react to damaged objects in different ways. Some decide to buy the damaged object in the hope that it can be restored; others shy away from this work and responsibility, preferring to only purchase items in very good condition. Which type of buyer you prefer to be depends on you, but here are a few points to think about while you make your decision.

☛ Take the age of the object into account. What is the likelihood of finding another example that has survived in as good or better condition?

☛ Has the price been fairly reduced to take the damage into account?

☛ Can the piece be restored? If so, will this be an easy and inexpensive process?

☛ If the piece can be restored, will the restoration lower its value?

☛ Is the object so rare or so essential to your collection that you'd rather have it in its damaged state than not at all?

☛ Are you going to keep the object and not sell it on? If so, ask yourself if you can live with the damage. If you can, save your money and enjoy the object as is.

☛ Do you intend to sell the object later on? If so, you should know that many dealers and collectors would rather see an object with all its defects and make up his or her mind on the restoration question.

☛ Keep in mind that the price of most restored items is about a third of their true value. If the piece is, however, extremely rare to the market—for example, a two-thousand-year-old artifact—most collectors will not be put off by necessary restoration.

☛ You will probably find that a good many items that you encounter in the marketplace have already been restored at one time or another. Indeed, in the 18th and 19th centuries, personal effects were highly valued, and even crude restoration was a way to keep an item in the family.

☛ If you do decide to go the restoration route, make sure to check that the restorer you choose is competent and knowledgeable enough to take on the job to hand. In other words, always use a professional. Every type of item has its own specialist, whether it be china, glass, silver, porcelain or furniture.

☛ Always consider the amount of the restoration cost against the true value of the restored item. If the former is more costly than the latter, you might want to think again.

Spotting a fake

It can be very disheartening to be busily amassing a fantastic collection when all of a sudden you find out that some of your favorite items in it are fakes! This gut-wrenching occurrence is best avoided altogether for obvious reasons. Drawing on my experience as an antiques dealer and in the salesroom, here are a few tips on spotting fakes that I've picked up along the way.

☛ Find out as much about similar items as possible, aka doing your research.

☛ Study the item in question and look for obvious signs of tampering meant to fool the buyer into thinking the piece is older than it really is. Check the interior and the base of the item for any deceptive markings. You should also smell the item, as pungent chemicals are sometimes used to age items.

☛ When buying at auction always read the catalogue description closely. If the description reads "in the style of" or "after," then the item is a reproduction.

☛ Consider the material, craftsmanship and style variations

typically associated with the object. Does the object that's under consideration look and feel like you think it should?

☛ If the price is inordinately low, you should be suspicious. Why is it so low? Is it the bargain of the century—or just a fake?

☛ Generally speaking, if the value of an item is high, or if the item is currently very popular with collectors, there will often be forgers out there trying to copy originals to sell to unsuspecting buyers. So beware of a marketplace suddenly flooded with a particular item.

☛ It may be worthwhile visiting a shop that actually sells reproductions of the item you collect in order to familiarize yourself with what a reproduction actually looks like. You could also try engaging the salesperson in the hope that you may pick up a few tips on the differences between the repro and the real thing.

☛ Always be sure to get a receipt from any seller. Authentic sellers ought to provide written documentation that states the age of the object and the price you have paid for it. If this is not forthcoming, be suspicious.

Rules to collect by

As you know, I have been collecting antiques—both of the present and of the "future" variety—for many years, and over this time I have learnt some valuable lessons which I would like to impart to you now. Here are my top five pieces of advice for beginning and maintaining virtually any collection.

1. Spend the most you can afford on the best possible example to get the best possible return. Here is a story to illustrate this point. In 1975, my friend David Dickinson was asked to procure a Minton Majolica Peacock for a client. Modeled by the sculptor Paul Comolera around 1873, it is believed that there are only eight examples of the Peacock in the world. David found one in Australia and procured it for his client for the equivalent of about $12,000. In 2006, the Peacock was valued at approximately $230,000, based on the retail price index. Not a bad return on an investment that was held and enjoyed for 30-odd years!

2. Sometimes it is worth selling a few pieces from a collection in order to buy one exceptional example. Many collectors will start out by investing in the more common patterns or designs within their chosen field, but as their knowledge builds, many will want to invest in better, bigger

or rarer designs. For example, my wife, Lesley, is an avid collector of 19th-century cranberry glass. A few years ago, it was becoming obvious to both of us that her collection was growing out of its show cabinet, but it wasn't until an impressive five-branch cranberry glass epergne was up for auction at an estimated selling price of $1,400 to $1,800 that Lesley thought of selling anything from her treasured collection. Within days, fifteen early purchases from Lesley's collection were entered into my next auction. None of the pieces she planned to sell had cost more than $50. With my help, Lesley raised just over $2,000 and became the proud owner of the cranberry glass epergne which beautifully adorns our dining table.

3. Try to avoid following trends in the marketplace, as prices for trendy items are often higher than they merit. Follow your instincts: if you think the craze for a certain object is a passing fad, then it probably is. Spotting the fads and changes in antiques is made easier by regularly reading the relevant periodicals, and keeping ahead of the game.

4. Seek advice from a friendly collector or expert. Asking these people questions will often reap huge rewards. Specialist dealers and collectors possess vast knowledge acquired by experience and time, and most will share their expertise with other buyers or collectors.

5. Keep a detailed catalogue of your purchases, including such information as when and where you bought the item and how much you paid for it. Keeping such a record will help you to monitor the item's increase (or decrease) in value, which is useful for price comparisons in the future. You should also keep a brief history of where you bought the item, how much you paid for it and any history particular to the item, such as that pertaining to its pattern, shape, number and designer. Yet another, albeit rather morbid, reason for keeping such a record is that upon your demise the inheritor of your prized collection will possess a detailed history for valuation purposes.

—Michael Hogben

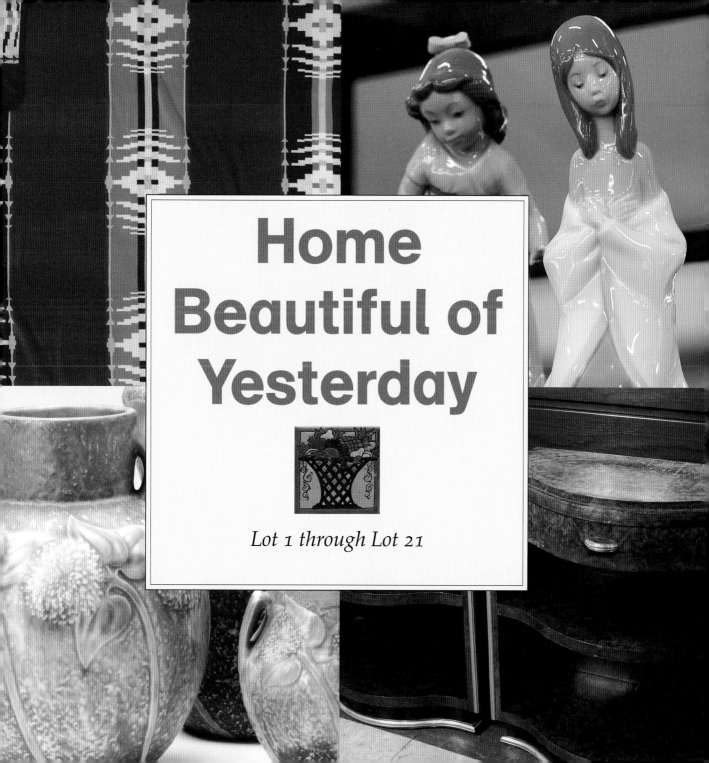

Home Beautiful of Yesterday

Lot 1 through Lot 21

Deco Wall Mirrors

The Art Deco period was a time of style and elegance, and Deco pieces are as fashionable in the home today as they were in the 1930s. Wall mirrors epitomize the angular elegance of that era. They are also relatively afford-able and eminently useful.

Bedroom mirrors were very popular in the 1930s, and some of the samples from this period have engraved or etched decoration. (Usually this decora-tion is comprised of a single section, but I have also seen some with several sections.) Vanity mirrors or shaving mirrors, though small, retain the style of the larger exam-ples, and have all the charm of the Art Deco period.

Keep your eyes open for mirrors with multiple glass sections. These come in sunburst shapes of all sizes, and most have clear, colored glass sections run-ning through them. Also look for rectangular and round designs; such wall mirrors were made in prolific num-bers and are readily available. The peacock-tail design—a large wall mirror in the form of a peacock's tail and similar to a hand fan—is equally collectible. Rarer are mirrors in the shapes of musical instruments, fish or boats; these will be harder to find and, accordingly, more valuable.

Items to look for

☛ Plain or etched small bathroom or dressing-table mirrors. Expect to pay $50 to $200; color panels add value.
☛ Medium-to-large wall mirrors. Expect to pay from $200 to $400.
☛ The most unusual shapes can cost up to $1,500. The best really are works of art.

Top tips

• Make sure that the mirror's glass is original by checking the color of each section. You will usually notice a different shade in any replacement glass.
• Look for a strong Art Deco feel when buying, as this will enhance the item's value.
• The 1950s and '60s saw an Art Deco revival, and many mirrors were produced in the style during that time. The only way you can tell the difference between these and the origi-nal '30s mirrors is by doing your research. Get the view of an expert if in doubt.
—M.H.

CARL WARREN

Lladro Figurines

Tipping future collectibles that are still being made is easier when the company behind them has a history of success with assured quality control. Lladro, whose well-designed porcelains are of consistent high quality, fits snugly into this bracket.

The Lladro company was founded in 1953 as a small family workshop in Almácera, a tiny farming community near the Spanish city of Valencia. Three brothers formed the company after having quit their jobs at the local tile factory. Their major piece of "machinery" was a small Moorish kiln they had built in the courtyard of their family house. The brothers quickly established themselves by selling their uniquely-styled, small porcelain figures at their local market. From these humble beginnings, Lladro now employs over 2,000 people.

Lladro porcelain is so popular that it is sold today in over 120 countries. Fortunately, Lladro's output is large because its figurines in the shapes of angels, animals and children have attracted thousands of collectors. The company also makes big figural groups to be used as centerpieces. Each piece has a charming title, often reflecting the pose of the figure. Every year new models are created, some of which are limited editions.

Items to look for

☞ Pre-1990 single figures cost $80 to $150; smaller items go for $55 to $80.

☞ Lladro figures made after 1990 are sometimes found for a fraction of their value at flea markets. I saw one sold recently for $15!

☞ Angels, young children and female figures are top of the list for many collectors. Expect to pay $125-$200 for one.

Top tips

• The history of Lladro's figures is well documented, and there are many reference books available, making it easy to research the date of your purchase.

• Always check the hands on human-style figures for damage; on animals, check the tails and ears.

• Nao is another brand name for Lladro that is used to sell cheaper versions of the company's output. While less costly, the Nao quality is still very good.

• The Lladro catalogue can be viewed online at www.lladro.com.

—M.H.

CARL WARREN

Head Vases

The best mid-century head vases are perfectly manicured and modestly jeweled models of ladies who lunched. The holes in their hats held water and flowers at bridal showers, charity luncheons and many other "affairs."

"I'm not sleeping in that room with all 'those people' watching me," a guest informed her hostess. Quietly sharing the guestroom was a collection of head vases. Even though "those people" were quite beautiful, and most had their eyes closed, the guest did not appreciate the company of the quaint, ceramic vases shaped—from the shoulders or waist up—as glamorous women.

There are head vases modeled on men, children, animals or cartoons, but the most collectible are the ladies who once graced party tables. Head vases were popular with mid-century American florists. There is a hole in the head of each vase to hold water and stems. Florists ordered vases by the dozens from wholesalers and importers. The vases also retailed for a few dollars each in department stores and five and dimes.

After they went out of fashion, old vases could be picked up for a quarter or two at tag sales. Early admirers snatched them up because a head vase was a useful and attractive collectible that didn't take up much shelf space. Years ago, Maddy Gordon picked up her first head vase at a flea market for under a dollar, and now has more than 2,500 in her Scarsdale, New York, home. The late Opal McCaslin of McCane, Kansas, managed to accumulate 1,000 of the vases in less than a decade.

Vintage head vases were manufactured from the 1930s through the '60s. Some faces were patterned after movie or TV stars, such as Marilyn Monroe or Lucille Ball. Usually, the head looked as if she had just visited a day spa—or what was then called a beauty parlor, with her bouffant hairdo, rouge-blushed skin and mink-like lashes. An intact head vase may show a lady with a short string of fake pearls around her neck and (sometimes) matching earrings. The most elegant vases feature a woman with a graceful hand, ending in red-enameled fingernails, cradling her chin. These are head vases with true attitude.

Although U.S. manufacturers created vases before World War II, in the postwar world, Americans could not compete with the Japanese imports, which also have value in the contemporary collectors' market. While the days of casually picking up a pretty head vase for a few dollars are history, desirable and inexpensive specimens still show up at the odd garage sale. However, in some areas of the country such finds are rare because head vases happily sleep in collectors' homes or else show up in small country antique shops. According to Dave Barrons, author of *The Head Vases by Numbers Price Guide*, a novice can find interesting vases for $65 to $125.

"LOT 3" PHOTOS BY BONNIE WOOD

A six-inch Jackie head vase, Inarco (1964)

Three American head vases display seductive eyelashes and other winning details. On left: vase manufactured by Enesco (1967); center: Inarco (1963); right: vase by Betty Lou Nichols (late 1940s)

Items to look for

☞ Betty Lou Nichols fired-up innovative and distinctive hand-made head vases featuring ladies with exceptionally long eyelashes, and gay '90s curly hairstyles under wide ceramic hats. Nichols' ladies also had, perhaps incongruously, fine manicures. Look for the artist's hand-done signature—BLN or Betty Lou Nichols or Betty Lou—under the bottom glaze. Betty Lou also named her ladies—Candy, Louisa, Valerie—so you may see, for example, "Louisa by Betty Lou Nichols" on the bottom of a head vase. Nichols' vases are usually in the $450 to $600 range, but price tags as high $2,500 have been affixed to a Nichols creation.

☞ Some of the oldest mass-produced American head vases were made by United China & Glass. They bore paper labels, marked "Ucagou." Other American manufacturers and their markings include Napco of Bedford, Ohio—look for paper labels reading "Napco Originals by Giftware." Some Napcoware signatures were ink-stamped and included a model number; on others, "Napco" was incised in the clay. National Potteries of Cleveland, Ohio, used the marking "Inarco." The face of the founder's wife, Roselle, is believed to be the inspiration for its vases marked "Cleve Ohio." It produced vases into the 1960s, including the desirable Jackie Kennedy look-alike. Prized Disney-character head vases were made by Enesco, which used paper labels.

☞ Many head vases were produced in Japan for pottery companies in the United States. Rubens incised its name on the bottom of vases it sold. Top quality vases from Relpo (Reliable Glass Co.) and Royal Crown were bottom-stamped in ink. Lego, Velco and Enesco bore only paper labels.

☞ Celebrity head vases—those showing Jackie Kennedy, Carmen Miranda or Marilyn Monroe—have zoomed in value. A Marilyn Monroe sold recently for $2,800.

Top tips

• Excellent condition: no chips, re-gluing, dirt or heavy crazing, no missing accessories, no paint loss. A head vase in mint condition is worth twice as much as a flawed one.

• Worthy accessories beyond jewelry include flowers in a hat or bows in the hair, gloves or umbrellas.

• Head vases are still manufactured, and reproductions of collectibles have emerged as prices have risen. As a new collector, arm yourself with the history of the vintage head vase. Consult books and make an online visit to www.headvase-museum.com.

• Size: Most 1940s and '50s head vases stand 6 to 8 inches tall. In the 1960s, Japanese makers cut costs and produced many vases 3 to 4 inches high. The taller size is preferred.

—L.A.

Mantle Clocks

*A*s early as the 18th century, clocks were placed on fireplace shelves. Today, old clocks continue to adorn the mantles and shelves of American and European homes. However, many handsome clocks from the 1940s to the '70s, have slipped past most collectors' eyes, making them ideal "under the radar" finds.

*I*f I'm right, I can see profitable returns in the coming years for collectors who get into good shelf clocks from the last century to now. Deco examples are an exception to the rule of unnoticed 20th-century mantle clocks. These are usually pounced upon when they turn up in salerooms.

Items to look for

☞ At the top end, luxury retailers such as Cartier and Japy Freres also sold mantle clocks of exceptional craftsmanship. These firms also made smaller versions of the mantle clocks, known as desk clocks. Depending on size and clock movement, such a prestigious clock will go for $500 to $1,000.

☞ The Swiss maker, Jaeger LeCoultre, is one of the top names in mantle clocks, and a clock with its name on it will cost from $600 to $6,000. If you have a healthy budget, I would recommend investing in Jaeger LeCoultre's Atmos clock.

☞ At the middle point in the market, look for strong shapes and designs, such as handsome display clocks in nautical style: a clock in the center of a ship's wheel, or in a dark wood case shaped as a boat. Some versions can also be used as wall clocks. Expect to pay between $30 and $75. An early-20th-century clock in a wood case with an etched-glass front might sell for $75-$200. A century-old brass and glass, or porcelain mantle clock: $500-$750.

☞ Quite wonderfully, some clocks in good-looking Bakelite cases can be found in the budget category. Other well-known makers, including Metamec, encase battery-operated clocks in vivid plastics. Many functioning, good-looking clocks can be had for between $10 and $30.

☞ Electric mantle clocks were a fad into the 1940s; many were shaped like classical clocks. These can cost up to $2,000.

CARL WARREN

Top tips

• Source your collection based on the principles of style, design and maker.

• The better the clock movement, the more valuable the clock will be. A faulty mechanism will devalue the piece.

—M.H.

Victorian Furniture

Victorian furniture began its second fall from fashion fifteen years ago. For this reason, I suggest that now is the time to reinvest in it.

If you're young, you may think of Victorian furniture as the antique choice of an older generation, and you'd be right. Victoriana faded out of style within a couple of decades of the passing of the grand old Queen herself, and languished until the 1970s when it became the affordable, stylish choice of younger people furnishing homes with a country touch. Its revival barely made it into the 1990s, and certainly the stuff was out of favor when this millennium began.

The price of Victorian furniture is now back down to what it was at the beginning of its first rediscovery period. When you can buy a good 120-year-old Victorian chest of two short drawers above three long drawers and with turned handles made by a great craftsman for about $500, you know it is time to snap it up. Rest assured that the Victoriana trend will return.

Items to look for

☞ Victorian pedestal writing desks. Made from mahogany, oak and walnut, the desks usually have twin pedestals, one on each side, containing a flight of drawers. You'll also want a leather tooled writing area. Try to secure one with the original leather. Expect to pay between $600-$1,000.

☞ Triple wardrobes. These beautifully crafted armoires have three sections to the front, and sometimes have mirrors on the interior doors. Expect to pay $600, or more than twice that for a large and fine specimen.

☞ Late 19th century: A sideboard or buffet will have a large mirrored back with shelving above a cluster of drawers and cabinets. Some even include a wine storage space. Those of classic Art-Nouveau-inspired design will sit well in any modern house. These are grossly undervalued and can be picked up for between $500 and $3,000 for a long, elaborately carved piece.

☞ Sets of balloon-back chairs. This usually durable and comfortable chair has a semi-circular back and a wide seat. The chairs can be bought in sets of 4, 6, 8, 10 and 12. When considering your purchase it is important to check that each chair is an exact match to the others in the set. For a set of 4 expect to pay $400; a set of 6, $800; a set of 8, $1400 a set of 10 or 12, $2000 or more. (A single ladies' (small) living room chair in the style—good for dressing table use—might be yours for under $100.)

Top tips

• Try to acquire solid, functional pieces of furniture (they tend to be better quality) in preference to veneered items. Look for solid oak, mahogany, walnut and birch.
• Check the item of furniture from top to bottom for woodworm! Also, look for alterations, especially to handles and feet.
—M.H.

Balloon-back chairs

CARL WARREN

Pendleton Blankets

The Pendleton Blanket is sometimes called an "Indian blanket," leading the uninitiated to believe American Indians made it. Untrue. Still, it's a good blanket—one that many Indians once bought and may still own, and one which some reservation stores sell today to tourists.

Mountain men such as Kit Carson traveled throughout the west and the Rocky Mountains, pulling beavers from rivers and bartering their pelts at Indian trading posts for silver accessories, tobacco, guns and knives. For many Indians, there were two important commodities to be bought at these outposts: Arbuckle's coffee and Pendleton blankets.

At the start of the 20th century, a wool mill in Pendleton, Oregon, (where sheep outnumbered people) produced durable blankets in bold, geometric designs that appealed to the Native American. The blankets were aggressively sold by Pendleton at reservations: to the Umatilla, Walla Walla and Cayuses of the northwest as well as to the Navajo of the southwest. Pendleton visited reservations to find out what colors and patterns residents preferred. The Navajo liked black, whereas the Crow preferred pink and blue. "The trade blanket is a

blanket made *for* Indians rather than *by* Indians," wrote David Friedman in *Chasing Rainbows.*

Indian children were wrapped in warm blankets. If a man was courting, he hid his head in a blanket as he walked through the reservation. If a man spoke in public, he wore his politically-correct "robe," i.e. blanket, before his tribe. Trade blankets became a measure of an Indian's identity. Even in death, his body was wrapped for a safe passage to the next world. "The blanket continues as a standard of exchange; and as a gift, the blanket is an important acknowledgment of friendship, gratitude and respect," wrote Robert W. Kapoun in *Language of the Robe.*

In 1923, President Warren G. Harding and his wife, Florence Kling de Wolfe, traveled to Meachem, Oregon, to dedicate the Old Oregon Trail. Indians presented Mrs. Harding with a woman's blanket or "shawl" in a white

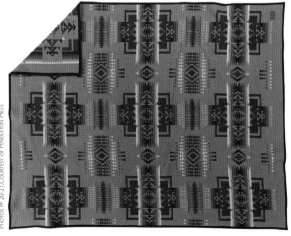

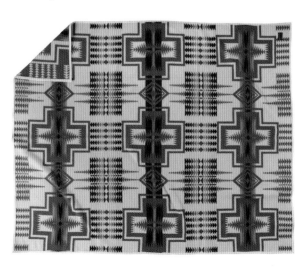

and pastel design, which was renamed "The Harding" in Pendleton's 1926 catalogue. It is a top collectible.

Although many manufacturers produced blankets after 1890, only Pendleton survived the competition. Its blankets of high quality workmanship and sophisticated Jacquard designs endured. Today, those vintage designs are spun on computerized looms. The new ones sell for $185.

Items to look for

☛ Blankets with rounded corners made between 1896 and 1908. These bear cardboard labels, and go for over $1,000 apiece, or as much as $9,500 for a one-of-a-kind design.

☛ Square cornered blankets manufactured in 1910, with vivid color and complex patterns. Expect to pay up to $6,500 for one in excellent condition.

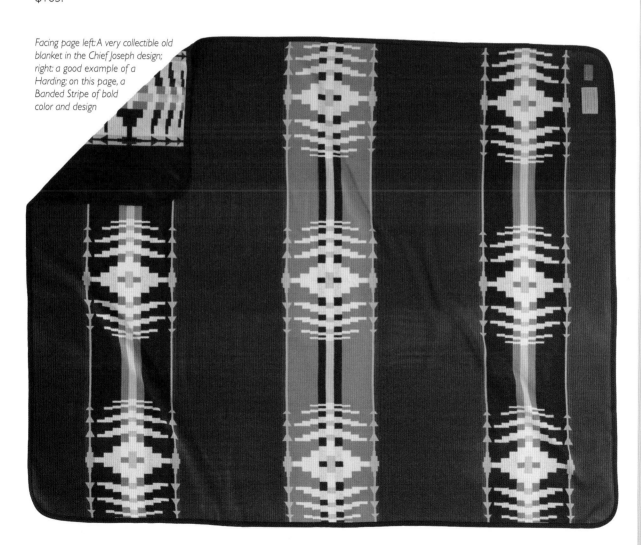

Facing page left: A very collectible old blanket in the Chief Joseph design; right: a good example of a Harding; on this page, a Banded Stripe of bold color and design

DAVID FRIEDMAN

A blanket known as the Dr. Whirlwind (1910)

☛ Bold primary colors, red and black, then blues and deep greens, are the most desired collectibles; earth tones and pastels are less valuable.

☛ The graphically smaller, more complicated patterns of 1920s blankets. In the '30s and '40s, the design scale became larger, using diamonds and large-cross motifs.

Top tips

• Mint condition is key. If you buy a blanket with multiple pulls, moth holes or burn marks, you're inviting a hole in your pocket.

• A genuine Indian trade blanket is 60 × 72 inches. Avoid blankets that have been washed and shrunk. They will have rippled edges. Look for intact binding.

• The cardboard label was followed by a stitched-in cloth label that read "Guaranteed to be A Pendleton—Pure Fleece Wool" or "Beaver State, Made by Pendleton Woolen Mills." Study up on labels before you buy. Since Pendletons are still manufactured, it's not always easy to spot a top-quality vintage one.

• Any good-condition Pendleton made between 1896 to 1942 is collectible; at auction or a flea market, most will fetch $250-$750 apiece. Expect to pay $750 for a good "Chief Joseph" from the '20s or '30s. Like "The Harding," the "Chief Joseph" can be bought new and perfect—a fine, warm blanket but not a collectible.

—L.A.

"An Oregon wool mill produced durable blankets in bold, geometric designs that appealed to the Native American."

Bamboo & Faux Bamboo Furniture

In the mid-19th century, imported bamboo furniture became fashionable in great American and British homes. Some credit a future King of England for setting the style; others say it owes something to returning missionaries. By the end of the century, both Europeans and Americans were pleased to be making their own.

In the early 1800s, the Prince of Wales, later George IV, bought bamboo furniture directly from Canton to add authenticity to the Chinese interiors of his principal residence, the Pavilion in Brighton. Bamboo was imported by businessmen throughout the century, or was among the possessions of Americans returning from China, but it did not stay chic.

A passion for Japanese art later in the century reawakened the western appetite for bamboo. In the United States, that enthusiasm was spurred by the 1876 international Centennial Exposition in Philadelphia. In some fashionable quarters, lacquered panels, rolls of matting and bamboo poles were imported from Japan. These were then made up into jardinières, pen holders, lamp bases, bookcases, side tables and even bedroom furniture.

Exports flowed from Asia but furniture factories in England also exported Chinese-style furniture. R.J. Horner of New York was both an importer of furniture from the Far East and a furniture manufacturer, producing his first Chinese-type pieces in 1890. Horner imports and furniture of its manufacture were sold from the Horner store on then-fashionable West 23rd Street in New York, and in other shops. Most "bamboo" furniture made in the west was faux bamboo. The French and English favored oak, pine and burl, but much American faux bamboo is of bird's eye maple. Americans liked simple designs to use in their New England summer houses. There are Victorian and Aesthetic Movement faux-bamboo examples.

Bamboo furniture dates back six or seven centuries to the Ming dynasty. Authentic old pieces can go for tens of thousands at auction. Some larger, intricately-carved mahogany pieces with the Horner label have fetched over $5,000 at recent auctions. Such pieces may be categorized as faux bamboo but, while they reflect Chinese artistry they do not look like genuine bamboo.

Traditional methods of bamboo construction are still being used. You should seek tightly-packed lattice work, a lacquer or cane work surface, banding and stretchers which continue around the outside of the uprights and wooden pegs holding all the joints.

Items to look for

☞ A two-tier, well-constructed end table. Expect to pay $125-$400.
☞ Chairs can be found for $75-$200 each.
☞ More unusual items, such as shelving and bookcases. Expect to pay $100-$200 depending on size. For a revolving bookcase: $600 to $1,500.

Top tips

- Bamboo is more difficult and expensive to repair than it looks so if the item wobbles don't be tempted by a lower price.
- Any damage to the lacquer will lower the price. Similarly, avoid any item that has been touched up with paint.
- Many items still have a maker's mark or label intact. These will be more desirable to a collector.
—M.H.

ALAN MARSHALL

Deco Bedroom Sets

*P*rices of *A*rt *D*eco bedroom suites have not zoomed, as *D*eco living room and dining furnishings and decorations have, possibly because many bedrooms are too small to accommodate comfortably these impressive suites.

*M*ost complete sets would consist of at least a double bed with headboard, two night tables (the nightstands may come attached to the headboard and bed), two armoires (one for the lady, one for the gentleman), a tall boy and possibly a wide chest of drawers as well, plus a lady's dressing table with attachable mirror, and a stool. An additional matching mirror is also possible. Some sets offer twin beds in lieu of one larger one.

The beauty of many suites emanates from its highly-glossed maple veneer, although other woods were used. Wood surfaces may have inlaid strips of another color, mirrored surfaces—clear or cobalt blue—and possibly also etched in the handsome spare Deco style. The more expensive pieces also have maple-lined drawers and interiors. The Art Deco theme is often seen most strongly in the handles and fittings.

It is not that unusual to see an entire bedroom grouping being sold for as much as only one or two of its pieces might fetch if it were broken up.

Items to look for

☞ An original bedroom suite from the 1930s with a strong design throughout. Expect to pay $500 to $800 at auction.
☞ Light oak, sometimes called blonde oak, suites are solid and well made. Expect to pay between $400 and $1,200 at auction.
☞ A 1950s version of an Art Deco suite will cost between $300 and $600 at auction. These sets are not, however, as well made as the 1930s sets.

Top tips

• Buying a complete suite can be cheaper than buying single pieces. Rather than sell off pieces, think about breaking up the set among rooms in your home. You might have almost enough furniture for two bedrooms, or be able to use the vanity table as a decorative desk elsewhere. If you have a walk-in closet, you might put your vintage armoires in the attic or the garage (storing your vintage clothes of course!). When, eventually, prices rise, you'll be glad you kept the complete suite.
• Look for a twin-pedestal dressing table with drawers in each wide pedestal, and a large circular mirror that attaches to the back of the dressing table.
• Bird's eye maple is especially desirable. A double bed with matching dresser in this finish recently sold for under $400.
• Make sure all the Art Deco handles and hardware are intact and match.
　　　—M.H.

"The beauty emanates from high-glossed maple veneer... the *D*eco theme is seen in its handles."

Deco double dresser and matching night tables

Barcelona Chair

Investing in a piece of furniture by German Art Deco legend Ludwig Mies van der Rohe is a serious move, and will take out a good chunk of your bank balance. But if you are feeling bold, you could see a major return.

The doyen of the modernist approach to furniture, Mies van der Rohe, was a leading exponent of the Bauhaus machine-age philosophy, famous for the dictum, "less is more." He was also a leading architect, creator of internationally renowned buildings such as the Barcelona Pavilion, the New National Gallery in Berlin and the Seagram Building in Manhattan.

From 1927 to 1931, Mies van der Rohe's furniture designs were manufactured by the company Berliner Metallgewerbe Joseph Müller, and after 1931, by Bamberg Metallwerkstätten. His furniture combines both classical and modernist elements, and achieves a machine-made look but with the luxury of a handmade finish.

Mies van der Rohe's most famous creation is, without doubt, the Barcelona Chair. Created in 1929 for the World Exhibition in Barcelona, this iconic chair is still popular and in production.

Van der Rohe also designed a Barcelona daybed, loveseat, sofa, two- and three-seat benches and a stylistically-similar coffee table. Knoll International holds exclusive rights to manufacture the Barcelona design.

Items to look for

☛ A Barcelona chair from the early years, 1929-47. You only want chairs from the companies then licensed to make them. In 1999, one vintage pedigreed chair sold at auction for over $9,000. However, not long ago, another seller parted with a pair of these chairs (without footstools) for under $3,000. Theoretically, a pedigreed, very-good-condition early Barcelona should now cost $15,000; the matching footstool: $5,000 but if you see the right chair in the wrong place, you never know.
☛ Today's licensee, Knoll, sells a new Barcelona chair for $3,900; the footstool for $1,800.

Top tips

• The first Barcelona chairs produced were unstamped and had no maker's mark. Buy this only if you're very knowledgeable and your seller is reputable.
• Always look for original upholstery, as this will be a major influence on price.
• In the USA and Germany it is actually illegal to call a chair a "Barcelona" unless it is produced by Knoll.
• In some places knockoffs abound; you can get the look on the cheap but not the investment..

—M.H. & L.A.

CARL WARREN

26

Eames Chairs

The husband and wife team, Charles and Ray Eames, was one of the more dynamic and talented design partnerships of the 20th century. Described by their friends as humanitarians, they wanted, above all, for their designs to be enjoyed as part of an "open, organic and emotionally expressive lifestyle."

Born in 1907 in St. Louis, Missouri, Charles Eames briefly studied architecture, but was dismissed for too fervently admiring only modern architects. He went on to study at the Cranbrook Academy of Art in Michigan, where he became head of the Industrial Design department. He married his colleague, Ray Kaiser, in 1941, and they moved to Los Angeles. By 1942, Ray Eames was experimenting with plywood, and had produced two organic sculptural chairs of plywood, evidencing her own interest in the avant-garde.

The Eames's first major joint project was their California home, which they named Eames House, Case Study House #8. The house was a perfect example of an economical space for both living and working, reflecting the modernist ideas espoused by the Bauhaus group and, of course, by the Eames. In the 1950s the Eames began designing what have become their famous classics: the Eames Lounge Chair and Ottoman (made in 1956 as a birthday gift for friend Billy Wilder, the film director), the Aluminum Group Furniture (1958) and the Eames Chaise (1968).

In 2008, the U.S. post office issued an unusual stamp with two faces—the Eames—on it.

Items to look for

☛ The Eames Lounge Chair and Ottoman. At auction, all depends on year and condition. Recently, a 1956 lounge and ottoman sold for $4,000, plus the buyer's premium. Another buyer snagged one elsewhere for under $3,500. New combos start at $3,600, depending on upholstery choice.
☛ The molded fiberglass seat on an Eiffel- tower-shaped wire base known as the Eiffel Chair. A 1956 Eiffel brought in $1,200 at auction but a 1963 chair sold for $300 at another location.

A new "side chair" in this style is $250; the "armchair" is $350.
☛ The Eames Child Chair: In 1946, the furniture manufacturer Herman Miller in Zeeland, Michigan, did a single trial run of this molded plywood chair, with a small heart-shaped cutout in the back. One of this group is displayed at the Museum of Modern Art (MOMA) in New York; another sold on eBay in 2007 for $3,750. Prototypes made in 1945 in Venice, California, go for more. A couple of years ago, the small chair was reintroduced in Japan.
☛ Plywood-and-steel storage units; the smallest unit can be yours for $250. Prices go up with larger configurations.

Top tips

• The year 2006 marked the 50th anniversary of the Eames Lounge Chair and Ottoman. In celebration, all chairs manufactured in 2006 featured a medallion affixed to the bottom, an unstated promise of higher future value as a collectible.

— M.H.

The Eames Lounge Chair (model 670) in black leather, first made in 1956

CARL WARREN

LOT 11

PH Lamp

Scandinavian designers have given us many modern classics, yet few pieces have achieved the international iconic status of the *Poul Henningsen PH* lamp.

Poul Henningsen was born in Denmark in 1894. He trained as an architect, but he soon became fascinated with the exciting then-new technology of the electric light bulb, and decided to dedicate himself to designing innovative light fittings. One aim was to recreate the soft gas lighting effect he had known as a child in a small town without electricity.

Henningsen experienced early success in his collaboration with Louis Poulsen & Co, a firm which sold tools and electrical supplies. They developed a hanging lamp and entered it in the modern lighting section of the Paris Exposition Internationale des Arts Décoratifs et Industriels Modernes of 1925. Based on scientific studies of light and shade distribution, the lamp was designed to avoid glare. Heningsten's design, known as the PH lamp, took first prize at the Exposition.

After the PH design proved commercially successful, Henningsen created other styles. Within a few years of the launch of the PH lamp, many Scandinavian homes and institutions could boast a Henningsen-designed lampshade. The PH shade is still in production.

Items to look for

☞ An original PH lampshade: Expect to pay $500 for a new one. Another option is to buy one secondhand for $100-$150.

☞ Henningsen's majestic artichoke lamp shade, produced in 1958: It is composed of leaf-like elements and, with its grand size, is ideal for larger settings. But unless you're lucky enough to find one in a family attic or in the garage sale of someone who hasn't done her homework, the artichoke lamp is as expensive as it is beautiful. The lamp is still produced in Denmark, and you can expect to pay $6,500 for the small one or $11,200 for the large one (not including bulbs) at Design Within Reach stores online.

Top tips

• eBay is the best place to look for a secondhand PH lamp shade. I recently secured one there for $130.
• Rewiring the lamp will not affect its value, and will make it safer to use. Try to use the original style wire, though!

—M.H.

A PH lampshade

CARL WARREN

Mod English Furniture

Two hot names for contemporary furniture collectors are British: Sir Terence Conran and Ernest Race. Acquiring pieces, especially early originals, will almost certainly eventually result in profit.

In the 1960s and '70s, Conran, with his Habitat stores, which included a New York outpost, was a leading retailer of modern furniture, and he shipped worldwide. The stores grouped furniture in lifestyle formats as well as by room, finishing each tableau with other for-sale home accessories. Conran literally created entire living areas which could be crated up and shipped wherever.

Ernest Race, while much admired by cognoscenti, has never been a storefront or household name. He started out in England, making inexpensive furniture from materials which were remnants of World War II. Race largely pioneered the use of steel-rod frame construction for chairs and couches meant to be outdoor or rec-room furniture. New York's Museum of Modern Art displays a chair of his design.

inside over the winter months if you want them to retain their value.

• It may seem obvious, but always make sure that any item you're considering is attributed to the designer in question. Until you're an expert, dealing with reputable dealers and auction houses is your best bet.

—M.H. & L.A

"Conran created living areas that could be crated and shipped."

1960s pine pieces by Terence Conran

Items to look for

☞ A 1950s white-painted metal rod rocking chair by Race. Expect to pay $400 to $800.
☞ An Ernest Race-designed steel and plywood Antelope chair, originally designed for the Festival of Britain in 1951. Recently, five chairs with one very small table were priced at $5,500.
☞ Nineteen-sixties pine furniture by Conran from Habitat. You could find a secondhand chest of drawers for $300; a side table for around $100.

Top tips

• Many Race items are designed for use outdoors, but make sure you bring them

Today's Top Chairs

Chair design changed radically in the last century. You can no longer judge comfort at a glance, and the "wow" factor in appearance is big. Architects and artists embraced new materials and high-tech manufacturing processes to remake the chair into eye-popping seating.

Left: the Sushi IV chair by the Campana Bros.; center: a Baas stool with pillow by Claudy Jongstra; right: the Favela by the Campanas

Most of us buy chairs to sit "in," and comfort is usually a priority. We eschew the upright, even elegant, chairs in our grandmother's house that seemed to force good posture and good behavior.

For design-conscious collectors, however, a chair is not just a rest stop but an innovative artwork worthy of museum space. Chairs by North American architects Frank Lloyd Wright and Frank Gehry are in the Guggenheim. The chair collection of the Museum of Modern Art (MOMA) in Manhattan includes seats from Ludwig Mies van der Rohe and Marcel Breuer, as well as the Eames, to name a few.

Now, the 20th century's sleek look of leather and steel has given way to materials you once would never have thought of sitting on, let alone slouching in. Serious chair collectors should take a look at the new work of some particular 21st-century designers: Fernando and Humberto Campana (The Campana Brothers) from Brazil and Maartin Baas from Holland.

Items to look for

☛ The Campana Brothers: Fernando, an architect, and his brother, Humberto, who studied law but had a passion for sculpture, founded their furniture atelier in the early '90s. The Sao Paulo studio produces vital creative chairs out of materials that most consumers throw away, including plastic bubble wrap, garden hoses, rope, fabric remnants, stuffed-animal toys, scraps of wood and cardboard. Some of their chairs look uncomfortable, but most are surprisingly accommodating to the human form. MOMA created a Campana exhibit in 1998. The talented brothers remain darlings of design, and if your wallet can take it, a Campana chair is a sound investment to sit on.

☛ The Campana Brothers named the Favela Chair for the impromptu dwellings of mud, stone and lumber scraps in Rio de Janeiro's sprawling shantytown. The Favela Chair (2002) at first glance seems haphazard, but actually is a construction of hundreds of pieces of irregular wood scraps, every piece hand glued and nailed together in a highly complex and precise design. Its price is anything but casual. Stand at attention for the $3,725 price tag! Hardly cheap, but it could appear a bargain decades from now.

☞ The Sushi IV chair (2003) is the fourth in a series of chairs with different shapes but similar coverings. Number 4 is a low slouching "drum chair," constructed of strips of felt, slivers of bright, Carnival-colored synthetics and pieces of under-carpet rolled together into concentric rings of upholstery over an iron base. The chair makes you happy just to look at it. This marvelous, funny-looking work of art is no joke. No more than 35 pieces will be made—only a few done each year—signed with a studio mark, and numbered per year of production. Each chair costs $75,000. Nothing fishy about that Sushi.

☞ Maarten Baas, a Dutch designer born in 1978, was an international star by the time he was 24 years old. His furniture design line called "Smoke," a series of burned-wood, handmade pieces, won him awards in Milan, Paris and London. Each mahogany, beech or walnut piece is strategically seared, and then sealed with an epoxy resin and/or a polyurethane lacquer. Baas' Smoke pieces look like props for the "Adams Family," and yet this burned furniture is eerily beautiful, even refined. Three years ago, Baas sanctioned greatly increased production of the line for hotels and art-gallery shops all over the world. Expect to burn through the bank account to buy one: $9,000 and up.

☞ Clay Furniture by Baas came to the fore in 2006. The sculptor created these chairs by hand-modeling industrial clay over metal skeletons, then painting their surfaces with bright primary-colored lacquer. The result deliberately resembles a chair that looks like a construction your third-grader made in art class. It has "naïve" whimsy and flair. The chair legs are not straight but purposefully shaped by Baas in a somewhat crooked form. In spite of this, the chairs stack easily and don't wobble when you sit on one. Look for a price tag of $2,800 each. A Baas clay stool topped with a pillow by Dutch designer Claudy Jongstra is $300 more.

"Baas created these by hand modeling industrial clay over metal skeletons, then painting their surfaces."

ALL PHOTOS IN THIS "LOT" COURTESY OF MOSS GALLERY

Clay stacking side chairs by Baas

Top tips

• Some Campana and Baas chairs are signed, limited editions. After the existing stock is sold, these items will go out of production, and come up for purchase only when an owner decides to sell. For designs not yet sold out, Gallery Moss on Greene Street in New York City is the exclusive U.S. dealer.

—L.A.

American Art Pottery

True art pottery is designed and hand-decorated by artists not factory workers. In the late 19th and early 20th centuries, American manufacturers hired local artists to work in their plants. This two-decade-long marriage of industry and artistry produced many objects of beauty.

LOT 14 PHOTOS, COURTESY OF RAGOARTS.COM

High quality work continued until World War I, but after the war the cost of producing works touched by the artist became too expensive for manufacturers to absorb. Most fine-art potteries ceased production, but not all. You can still find examples of excellent work created after 1915. A new collector should study the wide variety of pottery out there before deciding whether he or she wishes to collect by manufacturer, by year, by artist or even by color. Pottery is one collectible that you should make eye contact with—up close and personal.

Items to look for

☛ Roseville is probably the most widely known and most collectible art pottery. In 1890, Roseville—started in the Ohio town of Roseville—began making flowerpots, crocks, even umbrella stands. High quality lines designed by Frederick Rhead in 1904 are scarce and expensive, $2,000 and up per piece. However, by 1919 Frank Ferrel had created some of the pottery's most popular designs with relief-molded flowers and fruits. These patterns include Sunflower, Cherry Blossom, Wisteria, Dahlrose. Expect to pay around $600 for such a ceramic. Also desirable is the 1935 Pinecone pattern in green, blue and brown with an embossed pinecone and needles on each piece. Expect to pay about $1,200 for an item.

☛ In 1894, Newcomb College in New Orleans set up a vocational training program for young women artists that soon produced some extraordinary pottery. The ceramics were painted in a large college-created studio, not a factory, and sold in a connected shop. Between 1895 and 1940, ninety talented young women hand decorated some 70,000 pieces

A vase by William Hentschel for Rookwood

that had been crafted by male potters. The heritage of the Old South was recalled in the floral motifs on most vases—glazed with a distinct matte blue and green finish. Early works reflected earth tones: olive green and yellow. In later years, brighter over-glazes were used: cobalt blues, turquoises and soft pinks shimmer in these. Look for the logo "N" inside a "C," and expect to pay $1,500 or more for a fine example.

☛ Rookwood Pottery was founded by Maria Longworth Nichols of Cincinnati, Ohio, in 1880. The founder hired only accomplished artists to join her "pottery club." The club grew into a hugely successful business. One hundred and twenty artists and decorators were employed over its 87-year life. The firm developed unique matte and vellum glazes. Artists such as Jens Jensen introduced nude deco-like figures in the late '20s. Sarah Sax is known for her Art Deco style, Katoro Shirayamadani created spectacular dragon paintings and naturalistic leaves under a gloss glaze. Rookwood works are prized by collectors for style, consistent quality, exquisite decoration, and accurate

A collection of Roseville relief-molded Sunflower pieces (1936)

markings. Most per-piece prices fall between $800 and $3,000, but an extraordinary example can fetch over $10,000.

☞ The Van Briggle Pottery began operating in Colorado Springs in 1900 as a small studio run directly by the artist Artus Van Briggle, who had trained at the Beaux Arts Academy in Paris. Fortunately, he brought back to America his deft Art Nouveau painting style and his talent with matte

glazes. He is especially celebrated for his soft matte aqua colors, reminiscent of ancient Chinese ceramics. Van Briggle died in 1904, so the quantity of pieces hand-worked by the artist is very limited, although his designs are reproduced to this day. If you can find a Van Briggle "period piece," that is one created before 1912, you will pay $3,000 and up for it. But good, later reproductions of Van Briggle designs with embossed

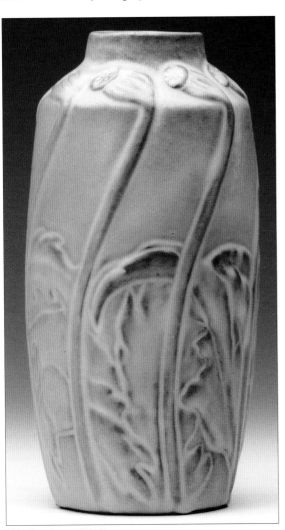

A Van Briggle vase (1905)

The bas-relief on this Weller century-old vase is known as the "knife-wood" pattern

leaves and flowers, under leathery glazes, are worthwhile at under $2,000.

☞ William H. Grueby is the King of Green and founder of the eponymous pottery firm. He created his signature matte green finish—a version of a French gloss, known as faience— in 1893. Although this now-famous glaze marks the majority of his pottery pieces, Grueby finished some works in other earthy colors. Beneath the glaze, Greuby pieces are decorated with hand sculpted forms, such as large ribbed leaves. Although a spectacular Grueby piece (shown in photo on the right) sold in September, 2007, for $70,000, examples of his fine-tooled designs can still be found in the $1,500-$2,000 range. His works were frequently copied and led to the closing of his studio in 1920. Grueby should be bought only from a trustworthy dealer.

☞ The Weller firm (1892 to 1948) in Zanesville, Ohio, made flowerpots, jars, jugs, and tiles. The company is best known for its Coppertone and Woodcraft embossed lines, whose pieces bring between $500-$1,000 today, and its more modern Hudson line, prized by collectors for its hand-done floral design. Hudson pieces go for between $3,000 and $4,000.

☞ Marblehead was a studio-art pottery in the Massachusetts seaside town of the same name. In 1904, Dr. Herbert Hall founded the studio, having decided that making pottery would be good therapy for patients in his sanatorium. In 1915, Arthur Baggs, an expert ceramist, bought the company. Marblehead was the most prolific producer of Arts and Crafts pottery in the 1920s and '30s. It specialized in works of unusual shape, with glazes that combined matte and pebble finishes. Blue was the most popular hue. Marblehead pieces start at $150, a comparative bargain!

☞ Fulper, in Flemington, New Jersey, is best known for an art pottery that it called Vasekraft, developed in 1909. Fulper utilized the then-new rich glazes that ran and seemingly blended colors into patterns on its Vasekraft vases, jugs, bowls and candleholders. The line remains popular although Fulper, which shaped its pottery in molds, failed to produce the consistent high quality of pieces made at Grueby or Rookwood, where ceramics were hand thrown on the wheel by master potters. The most collectible Fulper work has stained-glass insets or vibrant glazes. Such pieces start at $180.

Top tips

• Markings: Many distinguished potters had multiple marks, changing them over the years. The bottom of a pot can be ink-

A ribbed, matte green-glazed vase signed by William H. Grueby

stamped, die-impressed, trademarked, numbered, signed or unsigned, marked with a shape or raised form, or even have paper labels. It is worth buying a book on markings before you start to buy ceramics. Fake markings are common.

• Museum-quality examples: Some art museums across the country exhibit American pottery. High-end Grueby is sometimes found in such settings. The Philadelphia Museum of Art has spectacular Rookwood pieces and others in its collection. If you have a chance to train your eye by looking at great pottery, take it—even if you can't afford to buy a piece at a museum-quality price.

—L.A.

American Art Tiles

Watch out when you place your hot coffee mug on that tile trivet—you may be using a great collectible as a cup rest.

Over the past ten years, collecting tiles (once a small niche genre) has exploded as dealers have made more of the public appreciative of these decorative treasures. The Encaustic Tile Company started production in 1875 in Zanesville, Ohio. J.B. Owens began crafting exceptional tiles in 1885, and opened Empire Porcelain in Zanesville in 1923.

Most vintage tiles are clay—some were molded of damp clay, but many were formed from clay powders compressed into metal molds under enormous hydraulic pressure. Skilled immigrant craftsmen designed earthenware tiles modeled on European styles and employed Old World techniques in their decorating. An encaustic tile is one in which the surface pattern is comprised of different colors of clay, not glazes.

When Americans began to mass-produce pretty tiles, home builders and owners in the United States happily used them for fireplace and door surrounds, tabletops and kitchen backsplashes.

Many late-19th- and early-20th-century art tiles depict sentimental subjects—trees, castles, sailing ships, winsome animals—in soft colors. Some were finished with matte glazes, others offer bas relief under higher gloss.

Styles changed after the Arts and Crafts Movement shifted to the southwest and California. Highly collectible tiles from the '30s and '40s sport western designs in warm-sun hues. Other prizes are adaptations of Aztec and Spanish-Moorish designs.

Below: two Rookwood tiles, "Bird" (left), and "Leaves" (right)

The fruit basket and geometric tiles are by Empire; the tile below, picturing a sailing ship, is by Grueby.

Items to look for

 American Encaustic Tile Co. The firm eventually had plants in New York and California, too. You'll pay $55 and up for a single; $650-$5,000 for a fireplace set.

☞ Grueby faience, William Grueby, who in the 1890s worked in Boston, Massachusetts, created a signature matte green finish for his tiles and other pottery. Expect to pay a hefty $2,000 for a tile.

☞ A Weller tile, baked in Zanesville, Ohio: $1,500

☞ Rookwood in Cincinnati, Ohio, famed for its museum-quality (and priced) 19th-century art glass, also made tiles for major hotels as well as New York's Grand Central Station and subway stations. A single tile: $275-$350.

☞ Collectible California tiles include Batchelder—if signed, expect to pay anywhere from $100 to $1,500 apiece; Malibu: $40-$250; Claycraft, $60 to $2,000 for relief "scenics"; Gladding McBean: $50-$250.

Top tips

 Mint is a must. No chips, cracks, wear or trace of paint, grout or cement on backs or sides. Look for tiles that have never been set.

• The type of finish, whether high gloss or matte, does not affect value.

• Most pieces are not signed or marked.

• Look for old tile catalogues to find out where and when a tile was produced. Digitally-enhanced reproductions of catalogues are available from the Tile Heritage Foundation (www.tileheritage.org). Catalogue prices go from $10 to $100.

—L.A.

English Pottery

*W*ork from two English potteries is worth considering. They differ in period, look and price. Choosing is a matter of your taste and pocketbook, as both Ruskin and Wade pottery could prove sound investments.

The Ruskin Pottery was founded in 1898 near Birmingham, England, by William Howson Taylor and his father, Edward. That they took the name for the factory from the Victorian writer and critic, John Ruskin,

CARL WARREN

should tell you that they were aiming for art. The Taylors, inspired by 18th-century Chinese porcelains, experimented with flambé-glazed effects such as sang-de-boeuf, snake green and peach bloom. By 1910, they were visually successful and vases, candlesticks and plates with these finishes are very collectible and expensive.

Then recognized as one of the master potters of the modern world, William Howson Taylor built on this reputation, and kept his small team of accomplished potters working until 1933, adapting styles to suit public taste.

The Wade Pottery, founded 12 years before Ruskin, has gone through changes but still makes and markets work. I believe 1950s Wade will be an important area for the collector over the coming years. The 1950s graphics are standouts in strong colors including black and white, red and yellow. Many 1950 pieces were fluid in shape as were many of the clean designs on them. Wade's black and white Samba line boldly depicted tribal dancers on ashtrays, jugs and unusually shaped vases.

Wade's "Figural Cat" vases typify mid-century ceramics. Strong and highly graphic, the vase has four pronged feet and the interior is finished with red enamel. Wade pieces—including coasters and ashtrays—illustrated by cartoonist Rowland Emmet are also sought after.

Although not all Wade pottery is p.c. in today's light, Wade designs influenced others in ceramics, in furniture, in textiles into the 1970s, enhancing his pottery's value.

Items to look for

☞ Ruskin lustre ware, especially in lemon, yellow and orange. Expect to pay $400 to $1,400, depending on the size, style and

A Wade vase (circa 1955)

CARL WARREN

An assortment of Ruskin pottery with "flambé" glazes

decoration. A rare, 13-inch high-fired vase signed by William Howson Taylor sold for over $7,000.

☞ Any Ruskin piece inspired by the Orient. A six-inch vase with a delicate, vaguely Asian-looking grapevine pattern may be priced at under $150. However, many such items will be in the higher price bracket—$2,000 or more—they represent a good investment, nonetheless.

☞ Wade works: A Samba vase for $60-$75; Samba small items for $30 apiece; Figural Cat vases, $100-$160 for a pair; small pieces illustrated by Rowland Emmet, $10-$20.

Top tips

• When bringing the sort of money into play that a Ruskin would require, it is imperative to buy from bona fide dealers or auctioneers, as they will point out any restoration or damage.

• The majority of Ruskin pottery items were scissors-incised on the base with "Ruskin pottery" or "Ruskin."

• Restoration is, from time to time, acceptable with Ruskin pottery. The price of a restored piece, however, is reduced by at least two-thirds.

• Unfortunately, Wade's more unusual shapes are prone to hairline cracks, and the black enamel on the interior is prone to crazing and eventual peeling. It is therefore necessary to study the item carefully for signs of repainting.

• Check that the transfer on any illustrated Wade piece has no scratching and is generally in good order.

—M.H.

Lorna Bailey Ceramics

orna Bailey is an Englishwoman of barely 30 whose pop pottery figures have won the applause of her country-women who appreciate her timely, funky style. There is no reason why North Americans should miss this show.

I have no doubt that Lorna Bailey's designs are highly collectible as "tomorrow's antiques." Young as she is, her work has already spawned a collectors' club with well over a thousand members. While only a few American shops stock her, in this age of happy wanderers, not to mention those who travel mainly on the net, people almost anywhere can acquire one or more Bailey pieces.

Born in 1978 in Newcastle-under-Tyne, Lorna became a pottery collector as a child. After secondary school, she decided to study design at Stoke-on-Trent College. While she was still a student, a major ceramics factory, Woods & Sons, went into liquidation, and its assets were being sold. Luckily for Lorna, her father and a friend together purchased some of Woods & Sons' assets and took over a pottery, where they began producing hand-painted wares.

Lorna spent her free time painting traditional wares for the business, as well as experimenting with her own designs. Slowly sales of Lorna's work increased, and by 1998, Lorna and two members of the staff almost exclusively were hand-painting her stylish designs on vases, figurines and other pottery pieces. New pieces sell almost as fast as she can make them. At any given moment, there are likely to be four dozen Bailey pieces on offer at eBay, many of which can be bought outright. I think Lorna Bailey value can only continue to rise.

Items to look for

☛ The Astro sugar sifter. Commissioned in 1998 by *Collect It* magazine, Lorna created a limited edition of 250 sifters. The whole edition sold out immediately. If you can find a sifter, it will likely go for around $200

☛ Early pieces, such as original, shaped vases, can cost up to $800.

☛ Lorna has just produced some limited-edition figurines, including a series depicting The Beatles. These figurines now cost $60-$200, and their prices seem sure to climb.

☛ Refrigerator magnets are a bargain at $10-$15

Top tips

• All limited edition Lorna Bailey items will be numbered on the base.
• The more unusual the shape, whether a figurine or a vase, the more collectible the item will be.
• You can join the Lorna Bailey members club and receive special deals and editions that are only offered to its members. Check out www.lorna-bailey.co.uk.
　　—M.H.

CARL WARREN

Decorative West German Ceramics

LOT 18

Do you want to invest in the next big thing in the ceramics category? Then look at *West German* ceramics from the 1950s, '60s and '70s.

The unusual colors and bold shapes of these ceramics—mainly jugs and vases—should soon become instantly recognizable. Many have a volcanic look, with dripping, vibrant color and swirling or spider's web patterns. Also worth a look are the monochrome vases; these are usually embossed with geometric designs.

There were several West German manufacturers producing ceramics from 1950-1970. Many of these items can still be bought for under $40 but that will not be the case for long, so get in quickly.

Items to look for

☞ Pieces by Bay, Steuler, Scheuruck, Ruscha, Jopeko or Sgrafo to maximize your selling-on price.
☞ Larger pieces such as vases or centerpieces that are decorated with a range of bright colors. The maker is not so important as long as the piece is marked "made in Germany" or "made in West Germany." Expect to pay $50 to $120 for such items.
☞ Smaller vases, jugs or fruit bowls. These are currently abundant, so you can afford to be fussy with your choice. Try and stick to those in bright hues as these are generally the most valuable. Samples can be had for $30-$70
☞ Look for unusual shapes and patterns. A rare piece could be worth as much as $300

Top tips

• Look closely at the decoration, as the quality will vary.
• Always check for hairline cracks. This can be done with a flick of the thumb; if the pot sounds dead, then chances are it has a crack somewhere.
• Look for firing fractures in all large pieces of West German pottery. These were mass produced, and many suffered from substandard craftsmanship and inspection. Weak points include handles and feet.
• Some soldiers and their families stationed in Germany last century brought pieces home, as did some tourists, so stuff pops up at tag sales and flea markets here. European flea markets and secondhand shops are a boon for present-day travelers. Or you can stay home and browse eBay.

—M.H.

Scheuruck ceramic vase, jugs and corks

ALAN MARSHALL

Tools

About a million years ago, Early Man carved himself a pointed flint-stone to bash in the bones of a wooly mammoth. Early man's toolbox may have included stone knives, punches, picks, scrapers, axes, and even saw-like tools. Those items are now museum collectibles.

In 1942 archaeologists classified a site in Barstow, California, as a possible stone-tool workshop where, perhaps, early nomadic hunters and gatherers stopped to fashion and exchange their handmade tools. The first tool collectors club!

Today, the market interest in tools is emerging. Although men used to forage through garage sales looking for that much needed wrench or plane, the days of finding quality tools have long left the yard sale for the dealer's table, auctions and the Internet.

Tools are designed for different jobs; therefore, the variety is endless: braces, hammers, saws, gauges, levels, rules, shaves, anvils, plumb bobs, to name a few. Because of this diversity, tool collectors have established categories of tools to help them focus their collections. This goes beyond the function of the tool. Those who hunt only antique hammers, levels or planes must also refine their searches in other ways such as the material of the tool. Tools are made of various woods, steel, ivory, bone, cast iron, brass, etc. A rule collector may buy only ivory, boxwood or the rare ebony find. The plane collector wants only gunmetal but can afford only iron. Choose a catego-

ry and it will help you define and focus your own collection.

Items to look for

☞ Toolmakers: Collecting tools by the name of a particular company has become very popular and a common way to collect. "Stanley" is one of the most sought after names. The firm literally made thousands of tools of all kinds since the 1850s and also acquired its competitors whose names are synonymous with high quality. "Stanley Works" is still manufacturing today. Expect to pay anywhere from $50 to $500 for a collectible vintage tool. Other worthy makers include Davis and Stratton Bros. for levels, Underhill and T.H. Witherby for edge tools, Disston for saws, Norris for planes, Starrett for machinist tools, Coes for wrenches, Cheny for hammers, and Collins for axes.

☞ Tool Patents: Patented tools are the hot rage and fastest growing market. American ingenuity thrived in the 19th century and thousands of patents were issued, although not all made it to the manufacturing bench. Collect by type of tool, tools patented before a certain date, or tools patented by one individual or firm. Example: cast iron and hardwood hammer with rotating head marked "J. Lindley. Pat. Dec.2, 1890" sells for $330. Prices can go up to several thousand.

☞ Aesthetic Tools: These tools may function perfectly but are admired as art—beautiful pieces of sculpture. The tool, whether a level or a scraper plane, is carved from a high-end material

Below left: a knee brace for drilling holes; center: a "lady's hammer" used for breaking candy, patented by Charles T. Henning (1901); right: a brass bob (circa 1800)

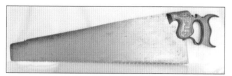

Antique saw (circa 1855) at left, and above, a close-up of its intricate handle fashioned by Thomas Tillotson; above right: an English mid-19th-century smoothing plane made by Thorne with a rosewood handle

such as ebony or rosewood; engraved; painted in floral or pin-striped designs. Integral parts are cast in filigree iron and sometimes "japanned" (lacquered) with a durable, black glossy finish. These tools bring top dollar—$700 to several thousand—at events. The world record for an ebony and ivory presentation plane stands at $114,000.

☞ Tool History: Some people choose to collect only by geographic or historical significance. Your hometown, state, countries, family names are popular. Others choose the Civil War era looking for wood molding planes or marking gauges, or decide on tools used in World War II to spear-point a collection.

☞ Miniatures: Manufacturers (Bluegrass, Hay-Budden) often made scaled-down models of their tools for their traveling salesmen to carry. Some tools are not miniatures but are just small in size, such as trammel points or plumb bobs. These tools are easy to store, taking up less shelf space in your home. They sell in the $100 range.

Top tips

• Condition and rarity affect the value in all types of tools. Keep the bill of sale or any paperwork on who owned the tool. It will enhance the value if you decide to sell.

• Avoid buying tools with rust, repaired finishes, stains or discoloration on wood or metal parts.

• Check the moveable parts: Do they work and have all their original parts and finish?

• Look for items in mint condition with the original box. A box can increase the value of your tool up to 12 times.

—L.A.

43

"Those who hunt only antique hammers, levels or plane must also refine thier searches in other ways, such as the material of the tool."

Watering Cans

I have been amazed at the price increase of garden-related items. Two years ago, it was rare to see watering cans for sale at antique fairs, yet today you will see them there being sold for $50 and more. Many people now use their gardens as living areas and so seek period decoration for them.

From the late-19th century until the 1940s, it was fashionable for manufacturers to produce specialist watering cans. Typically small, these were usually hand-crafted and intended for watering household plants. Many had an ornamental theme; some were even made in the forms of animals, while others were made with extra-long spouts. The vast majority of cans were made from galvanized steel or an alloy. The more costly can was one with an enamel finish.

Items to look for

☞ Late-19th- and early 20th-century cans in good condition are quite rare. Small decorative cans from this period can be worth anywhere from $50 to $150.

☞ Plain, standard-size models generally go for $30 to $50. Enamel-finished cans are worth $75-$135.

☞ Between 1930 and into the 1970s, most watering cans were made in traditional ways, but feel lighter to hold. These can be worth $30-$60.

☞ Edwardian-era water cans of brass and copper go for about $150. Brass watering cans from the first half of last century will generally go for $65-$100.

☞ Watering cans of the mid-20th century were enameled in various colors, including green, yellow, white and blue. These are worth $40-$80.

☞ Hand-painted and crested cans, or examples with advertising logos, are the top-end pieces for collections. These cost $150-$400.

☞ Shell, Esso and Castor Oil produced watering cans in the 1950s solely for the use of topping off radiators or cleaning window screens. Coveted by collectors, these cost $150-$250.

Top tips

• Make sure that the can still works, and that it has no stray holes or perforations.
• Check thoroughly for signs of repair or corrosion; both will devalue a can.
    —M.H.

CARL WARREN

Miniature Furniture

Originating in the 18th century but more widely available in the 19th and early 20th centuries, charming miniature pieces were a manufacturer's way of showing prospective furniture buyers a sample of the craftsmanship they could expect if they were to order the manufacturer's furniture.

Referred to in the antiques trade as "apprentice pieces" or "salesman samples," the reduced-sized items were, for all intents and purposes, an exact copy of their full-size equivalents, right down to the handles, locks and even the wood grains. Good miniatures were finely made by apprentice cabinetmakers under the watchful eye of the master craftsman.

Examples exist for virtually every type of furniture, including chairs, wardrobes, chests of drawers, bureaus, sideboards, beds and clocks, so for a collector the opportunities are endless. Sample-size furniture should not be confused with dollhouse furniture; an apprentice piece should measure from six to eight inches in height.

Items to look for

☛ Intricately detailed or very delicate late-18th- and early-19th-century models. A very special piece could go as high as $6,000.

☛ Late-19th- and early-20th-century models. A simple chest may cost $150; more elaborate and delicate pieces can go for over $1,500.

☛ Pieces by top retailers, as Asprey of London, who produced miniatures of a 1910 line are popular with collectors because of their superior quality. But you may pay up to $4,000 for a single piece.

☛ Early-20th-century models. These are often overlooked by serious collectors, so you can bag a bargain here. You could find something for $100; rarely would you be asked for more than $200.

Top tips

• Look at a miniature piece as you would any other piece of furniture: examine it for quality and look for signs of restoration.

• Look after your miniature-furniture collection as you do your real-life furniture: with a good coat of wax two or three times a year to enhance the patina and a gentle dusting every week.

• Never keep your collection too close to a radiator or other heater, or in direct sunlight.

• Housing your furniture behind glass offers good protection.

—M.H.

CARL WARREN

Keepsake
Art for Art's
Sake

Lot 22 through Lot 30

European Portrait Miniatures

Collecting portrait miniatures will bring out the detective in you, as much of the fun is in researching the sitter, and possibly the painter. Knowledge adds value to your collection.

Another factor influencing value is the frame: what it's made of, what work went into it, and its condition. Sometimes, what's most important is the material underlying the miniature portrait. Miniatures painted on ivory are the most prized.

Although portrait miniatures exist from the 16th-century, it wasn't until the 18th century that they became a must-have accessory for the rich and famous. By the late-19th century, the emergence of photography had rendered the miniature less desirable.

Research is essential when attempting to buy portrait miniatures. The quality and condition of the painting are initial considerations. If the portrait is unidentified, it may be possible to identify the sitter by visiting portrait exhibitions or looking at reference books. A knowledge of costume history is also necessary to date a miniature

with any degree of certainty. I would advise beginners to confine themselves to modest examples to start with.

Items to look for

☞ Genuine 18th-century portrait miniatures—English ones are especially valuable. Expect to pay $400 to a monstrous $60,000 for a fine portrait where both painter and subject are notable historic figures.

☞ Continental 19th-century miniatures are plentiful. Many European miniatures go for about $100 or less.

Top tips

• Inspect the miniature with a strong magnifying glass for any signs of restoration and any cracks.

• False signatures of well-know period artists are occasionally added. To be safe, make sure you are buying from a reputable source.

• Portrait miniatures by well-known artists often turn up framed in a square ivory frame made from old piano keys. Others turn up in a gilt metal frame with bows of metal ribbon decoration at the top. Such frames usually house contemporary copies.

• Beware over-painting on prints. Such fraudulent "originals" have often been placed in genuine 18th-century frames. This is when your magnifying glass counts. The best place to look for over-painting is under a spot of lighter color. Dark paints better conceal a printed line or stipple shading.

—M.H.

Stevengraphs

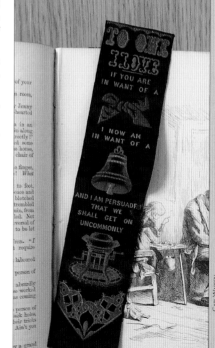

A Stevengraph is a small silk woven picture with elaborate patterning, fine detail and strong colors. They're made much the way fancy ribbons are. Most measure six by two inches.

Stevengraphs, produced by Thomas Stevens, were launched in great style at the York (England) Exhibition in 1879. The two silk pictures exhibited there proved incredibly popular: the first was called "London and York," depicting a well-laden stagecoach drawn by a team of four horses; on the mount were the words: From the Black Swan Holborn London to the Black Swan Coney Street York. The second picture was called "Stevenson's Triumphs, 60 miles an hour" and showed the train, "Lord Howe," pulling two carriages. Early examples of both images bear the "York Exhibition 1879" monogram.

A stream of silk pictures soon hit the market, showing famous buildings, sporting and historical scenes, and portraits. Stevens also produced relatively affordable silk bookmarks—some precede his great York success. The grandest and largest Stevens ribbon was the Great Sash for the Ancient Order of Foresters. The design was registered in 1873, and measures seven feet by six and a quarter inches.

The market for Stevengraphs has subsided over the last 15 years, and prices are very approachable, especially for his shorter ribbons in honor of a person or occasion. This is a collectible that's easy to transport or ship. The term "Stevengraph," has come to refer to all Victorian silk image collectibles. Most actually made by Thomas Stevens were marked: Woven in silk by Thomas Stevens. They're so numerous, I'd suggest targeting a specific Stevens subject. But you might also choose to collect similar ribbon pictures made in England or Germany.

Items to look for

☛ Bookmarks: Recent price-points in the U.S. include $65 for an 1870s "Remember Me" Thomas Stevens silk strip, and $550 for an 1893 weaving showing London's famous Crystal Palace.

☛ Portraits. Expect to pay $20-$80.

☛ Landscape views in original frames and in good condition. Expect to pay $60-$180.

☛ Horse racing scenes for $120-$160; bullfighting, rugby or Victorian cycle races for $200-$450; most other sports for $120-$240.

Top tips

• Look for clean, undamaged pictures with strong color.

• A remounted Stevengraph will be less expensive, unless it is a very rare example.

• Never reframe a Stevengraph; keep it in its original gilt frame if possible.

• Keep all color silk pictures out of direct sunlight.

• If you intend to collect the Stevengraph bookmarks, make sure the tassels, if any, are intact.

—M.H.

Small Stevengraph ribbons make ideal bookmarks.

49

Art Nouveau & Deco Postcards

ollecting postcards was a hobby so popular at the turn of the 19th to 20th century that more postcards were mailed in the United States (about 700 million) than the total of its population (89 million). Back then, most postcards purchased in the United States had been imported from Europe.

Postcard collecting became a hot hobby in 1889 at the Paris World's Fair when 300,000 souvenir postcards illustrating the new Eiffel Tower were sold to visitors. Soon, postcards picturing other wonders—manmade and natural—were being collected. Postcards

communicated to Edwardians the way television communicates to the modern world. They commented on many aspects of society and illustrated "progress" to millions of collectors.

Today, collecting vintage postcards is a fast growing area of the ephemera market. Some collectors specialize in documentary postcards on a topic, such as photos of roadside diners, landscape scenery, or transport from horse and buggy to airplanes. The cards I'm focusing on here are the most highly-designed ones—small canvasses in the Art Nouveau style (1895-1910), rooted in Paris and Vienna, and Art Deco cards of the 1920s and 1930s that reflect the high-style design of that era.

Postcard printers were a big force behind the Art Nouveau cards. The postcard manufacturers wanted to attract the public to their new product, and so hired artists whose work reflected the new, elegantly fluid style to create impressively beautiful cards. Rather quickly, high-quality artistry began to appear on commercial postcards advertising everything from liquor, biscuits and cigarettes to theatrical productions. Many such cards are gems, small oblongs of lithographed pasteboard that preserve a bit of an era and a genuine artistic expression of it—at an affordable price. Unlike buying a painting, you won't have to break your bank account to collect many of these tiny artworks.

Items to look for

☞ Cards by Alphonse Mucha: In 1894, this obscure Czech painter and illustrator soared to stardom when his spectacular nearly life-size posters of actress Sarah Bernhardt in her leading role in the play, *Gismonda*, went up in Paris. The Art Nouveau movement was born, with Mucha as its most important exponent. The Gismonda poster won raves on its own, and Bernhardt rewarded Mucha with additional contracts. Other impresarios signed Mucha to design sets and costumes, jewelry and even book covers, as well as more posters and postcards. Recently, a small Mucha poster, "JOB," sold for over $26,000. But you can buy a postcard with the same design elements: those sensuous curves depicting women in neoclassical robes whose twisting hair mimics vines. Expect to pay $1,000-$2,000 for a genuine period postcard.

☛ Collecting postcards was a hobby so popular at the turn of the 19th to 20th century that more postcards were mailed in the United States (about 700 million) than the total of its population (89 million). Back then, most postcards purchased in the United States had been imported from Europe. Cards by Raphael Kirchner: This Austrian portrait painter and illustrator moved to Paris around 1900 and became one of the more celebrated artists of his time. Kirchner designed a wide variety of advertising postcards but is probably best known for his risqué illustrations of women. Kirchner's Art Nouveau pinup girl was said to be inspired by his wife Nina. Kirchner's iconic naughty women were much sought after by World War I soldiers. Kirchner designed 1,000 different postcards. His "geisha girl" series was so popular they were reprinted four times for a total of 40,000 postcards. Most Kirchner postcards sell from $40 to $160, but some rare cards can fetch $350-$750 apiece.

☛ The exaggerated drapery look of Art Nouveau gave way to the severe stylized lines of Art Deco during the roaring '20s in Paris. Although production of art postcards had dropped significantly after The Great War ended in a shaky peace, a

French-made postcards, by Czech artist Alphonse Mucha, on the facing page and left and right of this page, typify Art Nouveau; the center card, by Austrian painter Raphael Kirchner, depicts a charming pin-up girl.

The naughty Deco card at left is by Umberto Brunelleschi; below are two romantic Giovanni Meschini cards. The two lovely cards are in the facing page are also by Meschini.

small group of Italians continued designing such cards. They represent, as one historian put it, "the last flowering of the Golden Age of postcards." Their superb postcards, often stenciled, built their sophisticated design on solid blocks of color. Look for cards carrying the credit of Giovanni Meschini, Loris Ricco, Marcello Montedoro or Umberto Brunelleschi. Top condition cards go for $85 and up.

Top tips

- Seek near perfect condition in a postcard. Creasing, staining or damaged corners significantly reduce value.
- Some artists signed their work; signed cards are more valuable than unsigned postcards.

- Postal rules of the time allowed only an address to be written on the flip side of a picture postcard, so senders often wrote on the image. This does not necessarily decrease a card's value.
- Use acid-free paper to separate the postcards in your collection. Store cards away from sunlight in a "standing-up" position (short end down), as stacking them causes damage.

—L.A.

Tobacco Silks

Competition sometimes breeds creative advertising. Tobacco companies, back in the early 1900s, enticed customers to buy particular brands by inserting a small, attractive collectible into each package of cigarettes—a "silk" about 1 x 3 inches. These small, imprinted textiles became known as "tobacco silks."

The first silks were of a series of sports figures—an idea that would morph into sports trading cards. Tobacco companies also devised tobacco-silk series aimed at women. It was a good way to build brand loyalty and to keep customers coming back for more. Smokers, both men and women, could aim to collect complete sets of various designs.

The tobacco companies encouraged women to collect the silks by distributing instructions on how to make them into pillow covers, purses, tablecloths, clothing items, quilts and curtains. If you smoked enough you could also collect coupons that would entitle you to redeem your coupons for a 24-inch square pillow top cover. That would cost you 60 coupons and a lot of inhaling.

The single silk portrait survives as the better collectible since the sewing skills of the women who made these patchworks were not always up to snuff. A good quilt is a rare find. The practice of including silk novelties in cigarette packets diminished with the beginning of World War I. Though their window of production was short, the combination of addictive pleasures—smoking and collecting—assured that many of these small and delicate novelties survived.

Items to look for

☛ A tobacco silk was always called "silk", but they were actually made in a variety of fabrics: combinations of silk, satin, cotton and flannel.

☛ After World War I, European, particularly British, tobacco companies adopted the tobacco silk—by then the silk was a polychrome printed on one side like a photograph. Usually, the name of the tobacco company was also printed on the fabric.

☛ Collect by theme. It will make your life easier as there are dozens and dozens of subjects. Today, a college-sports silk, depicting a top college athlete—a runner or rower, for instance—and the name of his college, sells for about $10 each. Singles at the same price level can be collected from series as diverse as popular actresses of the time, bathing beauties, national flags, animals, monarchs, generals and popes.

☛ Kensita Cigarettes issued a series of tobacco-silk flowers which were popular because each came with a little history of the blossom. These now sell for $20 each.

☛ American Indian chiefs are harder to find and so each one costs more: expect to pay $35. Larger silks sometimes are sold in sets for as much as $150

☛ Old tobacco names such as: Zira, Nebo, BDV, Piedmont, to pinpoint a few.

Top tips

• Good condition. These silks easily fray at the edges and require gentle handling or framing.

• Look for a clear picture without fading or folds.

• Avoid buying silks with "foxing"—brown or brownish red spots caused by mold or oxidation of iron particles—as this will diminish value.

—L.A.

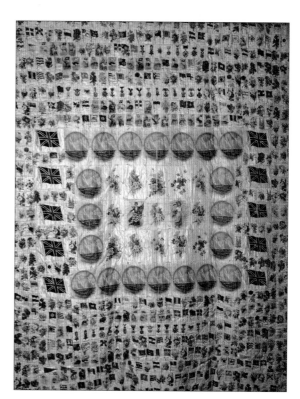

A series of bathing beauties, a series of Indian Chiefs and, at right, a 1915 British tobacco-silk quilt

Vanity Fair Illustrations

Chic *Vanity Fair* has been the magazine that would not stay dead. Born in America in 1858 as a humorous publication, it was killed in 1865 by the solemnity of the Civil War, but a magazine of the same name, devoted to the wellborn and well-known—society—arose in London in 1869, where it flourished until felled by World War I. Never mind. As it was dying over there, over here, the dapper Condé Nast was bringing *Vanity Fair* to life.

The Americn *Vanity Fair*, which was resurrected in 1914, died again in 1936, at the bleak heart of the Depression. The glib sleeping beauty was reawakened in New York in 1983 by the corporate Condé Nast, and it's still kicking up its heels.

What most interests us here are the caricatures *Vanity Fair* published during its London heyday and in its early-20th-century American revival. On either side of the pond, most *Vanity Fair* caricatures were of well-known figures of the day, and most were not flattering. Several of the cartoons had a life as lithographs before and beyond the monthly magazines.

What actually appeared in the magazines, of course, was printed. Most, except for cover illustrations, were black and white. In the old-print marketplace, however, old chromolithographs and sometimes hand-colored engravings and lithographs of what was once published in black and white can be found. Much of the available art derives from the British *Vanity Fair* but there are also American treasures to be had. Some Ashcan artists contributed to the early-20th-century U.S. *Vanity Fair*—their sensibilities were a match!—and their more serious students also contributed, such as William Gropper, whose early 1930s caricature of Emperor Hirohito of Japan got him labeled as "prematurely" anti-Fascist.

If you seek cover lithographs, keep in mind the measurement of the old American *Vanity Fair*: 9.5 × 12.5 inches.

The difference between *Vanity Fair* from London and *Vanity Fair* from New York often seems unclear. For instance, in 1872 the British *Vanity Fair* commissioned from the well-know American caricaturist Thomas Nast (who worked principally for *Harpers Weekly*, and immortalized Santa Claus in a red suit) a series of caricatures of political figures. Of course, there was no American *Vanity Fair* in that decade.

Nicely hand-colored illustrations of sporting events, including days at the races, and images of cultural and political get-togethers are available. If you find yourself staring at an illustration of a cricket game, you can be pretty sure it wasn't published in the American *Vanity Fair*.

The market value of *Vanity Fair* art has fluctuated over the years. With their value now at an approachable price, I think it is time to buy.

Items to look for

☛ Sporting prints are very popular. Expect to pay $75 to $150 depending on the subject matter. A large, hand-colored lithograph of an American race scene sold recently for $195.

☛ Caricatures of famous politicians are prized. Expect to pay $100 or more for an unframed print, accompanied by a short, humorous biography.

☛ A color unframed lithograph of Hirohito by Gropper was offered not long ago at $485.

☛ Try to collect themed sets. Pre-1900 individual prints from the English *Vanity Fair* are desirable at about $200 apiece, unframed.

Top tips

- Steer clear of reproduction prints as these are not a good investment.
- Original 19th-century lithographs will have a plate line on the exterior of the color print. Many caricatures have short humorous biographies with them. They should be complete, in their proper place, for full value.
- It is essential that the print has no tears or fold marks.

—M.H.

World War I Posters

*T*here was a time when posters did more than advertise; they inspired us with powerful propaganda. *A*merican wartime posters urged everyone to participate in the war effort.

58

*P*osters are so common in our lives that we go on our daily rounds, scanning the ads for Gap T-shirts or Chanel perfume or a *Nutcracker* ballet performance with unconscious recognition. But when posters were not so common, they had even greater power. World War I posters recruited men into the armed forces, urged women to support their troops, sold war bonds to civilians, reviled the enemy, and demanded Americans give their "all"—their time, money, even food, to the cause.

In 1917, the federal government recruited artists and commercial illustrators to design posters supporting the United States in what was soon known as The Great War. Today, these World War I posters have signif-

icant value. In fact, these striking posters were instantly popular. The public loved the patriotic rally and they loved the tens of thousands of war posters pasted to the walls of libraries, schools and post offices from coast to coast.

The artwork was colorful, artistic in design and meaningful. "Eighty years after the government printing office released these posters, they've become a collector's dream," says Nicolas Lowry, poster appraiser for Swann Galleries in New York. "There are more posters than there is the demand right now. The right time to buy is now."

Items to look for

☞ Howard Chandler Christy was one of two top illustrators who set the gold standard for World War I posters. When the U.S. entered the fray, he was already famous for his paintings of "the Christy Girl," a charming, romantic-looking young woman similar to the Gibson girl. His wartime posters depict various incarnations of the Christy girl as nurse, Liberty, or Justice. One lovely poster shows a girl wishing she could join up as a sailor. An original in good condition will cost you $1,500-$2,000.

☞ James Montgomery Flagg originated the now-iconic "I Want You" poster, showing a grim Uncle Sam pointing to the viewer, with his demand. This legendary poster in good condition costs $15,000; in poor condition it's $1,300, but probably worth it. Flagg also designed a sleeping Columbia, wrapped in her flag gown, while fire rages behind her—a wake-up call to America. Flagg's Columbia fetches $7,000 or more. But you can find many other good war posters by Flagg for about $1,000.

Most propaganda posters of the First World-War era by other illustrators will cost between $175 and $800.

Top tips

• During the war, the posters were printed on cheap paper and not expected to last more than a few months. Look for top condition, no significant tears or paper loss and vibrant color.

On left page: two posters by Howard Chandler Christy, showing Marines (1915) and Navy (1917); this page: poster by James Montgomery Flagg (1917)

• Slight creases or blemishes are acceptable.
• Avoid posters with heavy restoration, pronounced amounts of fading and discoloration.
• Beware of reproductions sold online for $15 to $50. You may want them for their design quality, but they are not going to increase in value like an original.

—L.A.

Animation Art

The creator of The Simpsons, Matt Groening, once said, "There's no amount of money that an animator can be paid—they deserve our eternal gratitude."

Left to right: hand-painted cels from Flintstones *"Art Class;" "Love in Bloom," Disney; Lisa and Homer of* The Simpsons.

In this age of computer-generated cartoons, we can only look back on the time of hand-drawn animation with absolute, awestruck wonder. Each cartoon character was assigned an animator who created pencil drawings (also collectible) of its expressions and actions. Finished drawings were transferred to cels—a cel is a single sheet of clear celluloid.

Inkers traced the character's outline on the cel front; painters colored in the characters on the cel back. Multiple cels were layered—character cels with foreground and background cels. Hundreds or thousands of cels were photographed in sequence to make moving cartoons. In the late 1930s, it took almost 1,500 cels to make one minute of a Walt Disney animated film.

When you buy an original cel, you are purchasing a lost art form. Unlike computerized animation, a vintage cel is a little handmade masterpiece. The subject of a cel can add star quality, which is to say you want Snow White rather than a dwarf, Pinocchio rather than his father. More complex imagery on a cel also raises its price.

Items to look for

☞ Limited edition Disney cels, 1937-1967. These make collec-

tors pant. Cels from a famous film that feature its lead character in a memorable scene bring in big bucks. After that, the more complex the scene the more a cel is worth. Cels of Mickey Mouse in *Fantasia* doing his Sorcerer's Apprentice scene have gone for $35,000 each. A cel brimming over with black and white puppies from *101 Dalmatians* sold recently for $12,000. Expect to pay more like $400 to $8000 for most numbered Disney cels.

☞ Original production drawings. These were the final black & white drawings for cels. Expect to pay $300-$2,000.

☞ Sericels: Cels printed by serigraphy on clear acetate and produced by the thousands, often for giveaways to crew members and office clerks: $150 -$300.

☞ Warner Brothers cels, 1930-1950: Cels of Bugs Bunny, Daffy Duck, Road Runner and Elmer Fudd, by Chuck Jones; cels of Sylvester and Tweety Bird by Bob Clampett, $600-$1,200. MGM cells from *Tom & Jerry* by Joseph Barbera; cels of Popeye or Betty Boop by Max and Dave Fleischer, $125-$800.

☞ Modern cels: From *The Simpsons* by Matt Groening, $15--$1,400; Charles Schultz's *Peanuts*, $1,200-$2,000; *The Flintstones, The Jetsons* or *Yogi Bear*, all by William Hanna and Joseph Barbera, $175-$1,000; cels from *The Little Mermaid* by Ron Clements and John Musker go for up to $1,400.

☞ Modern Disney lithographs: A single character, such as the Little Mermaid, can go for as little as $25.

Top tips

- Top condition plus: You want the image of your favorite cartoon mouse or rabbit beaming at you. That means eyes open are worth more than characters with eyes closed. It's all in the details.
- An authentic cel should come with a certificate, a seal on the cel and a number certifying that it came from a film studio like Disney or Warner Bros. A reputable dealer will have those certificates. They are licensed by the studios to sell them.
- The gouache paint tends to chip and fall off the celluloid. Missing color dramatically decreases value.
- Most cels are not signed by the artist.

—L.A.

Above: Two giclees on paper, signed by Toby Bluth, done for Snow White, *Disney (1937), below: two original production drawings from* Sleeping Beauty, *Disney (1959)— on the left is Maleficent, and on the right Maleficent, after she has turned herself into a dragon.*

Zulu Wire Baskets

Collecting modern Zulu baskets (those made in the last 50 years) opens up great possibilities for colorful display, and expresses an eco-friendly attitude. If you include beautiful new baskets, which are well worth having, you will also contribute to the livelihood of South African weavers.

For centuries, the Zulu have been using their artistry to weave baskets out of grasses and palm leaves. The baskets were so tightly woven, some were used as lids on the highly-polished clay pots that stored their homemade brew.

In Zulu culture, strict rules are followed in the drinking and presentation of their beer. A bride gives her new in-laws a set of beer pots and *imbenge* (wire) baskets, in honor of ancestral spirits and to bring dignity to the home.

This age-old craftsmanship of weaving grass baskets has been applied to a new medium. In the late 1960s, technology brought with it new materials such as plastic-coated telephone wire. Factory night watchmen

This South African basket is 12 inches in diameter.

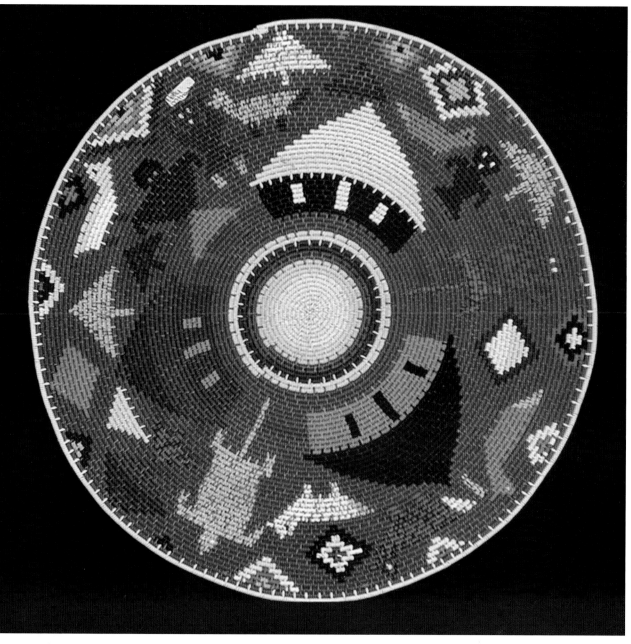

Pictorial basket by Nelly Mthembe.

picked up plastic wire scraps and wove them around their traditional sticks—just to pass the time. The practice gained popularity in Zulu communities. Bright and colorful wire lent itself to the creation of bold designs and swirling patterns. Many men and women adapted traditional grass designs into new, original works. Telephone wire baskets have now moved from impoverished rural villages of South Africa to exhibitions at the Smithsonian. Contemporary artisans produce baskets "as thin as the finest grass, stronger than palm leaves, and more colorful than the best dyes obtained from local

roots and leaves," according to a spokesman for the Museum of International Folk Art in Santa Fe.

Items to look for

☞ Wire weavers make their baskets in two ways. In the hard-wire technique, a weaver starts with a spool of galvanized-steel wire. As a craftsman unwinds the thick wire, he or she twists thinner colored telephone wire in tight loops around the galvanized steel, binding the two kinds of wire together. This technique is as old as the African grass basket. Steel substitutes for grasses and the thin wire replaces palm leaves. The basket is very strong, and supports great design variety. The soft wire basket-making technique borrows shapes. Wire is braided over a bowl or a plate and then the "mold" is removed. Both basket types are collectible.

☞ Because these baskets are hand-woven, each one is distinctive. Patterns may incorporate small houses, complex geometrics, zigzag designs, flowers, human figures and indigenous animals.

☞ Cooperatives in South Africa sell their works to retailers around the world. Look for baskets tagged by Bartel Arts Trust (BAT) with the names of the artists. Representatives of the BAT cooperative appear every July at the International Folk Art Market in Santa Fe, New Mexico. For information, but not shopping, you can visit its website: www.folkartmarket.org.

Look for the work of renowned contemporary basket weavers such as Vincent Sithole, Zama Khanyile, Mboniseni Khanyile, Ntombifuthi Magwasa, Elliot Mkhize. Expect to pay $1,000-$2,000.

☞ You can purchase many baskets woven by less established artisans such as Zodwa Maphumulo, Mathungo Thabede, Nelly Mthembe and Buthelezi Shange for $25 to $285. Price depends on complexity of design and size of the basket.

Top tips

• Clean wire baskets with cool soapy water and keep away from sunlight and heat.

—L.A.

Page 64: A 9-inch high, foot-wide conical basket

This page: The basket at left with the swirl design basket is only 7 inches wide. On the right is a shallow, woven bowl by Zodina Maphumulo, one-foot wide at its top.

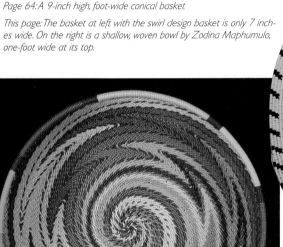

"Bright and colorful wire lent itself to the creation of bold designs and swirling patterns."

Vasarely Silkscreen Prints

Hungarian artist and architect Victor Vasarely is considered by many to be the inventor of "Op Art." Although his work is not to everyone's taste, his vibrantly colored silk screen prints are both stunning and highly collectible.

Born in 1906 in Hungary, Vasarely studied applied graphic art and typographic design in Budapest. He left Hungary for Paris in 1930, where he worked as a graphic artist and creative consultant for an advertising agency. In 1938 he created what is considered the first true piece of Op Art—"Zebras" a canvas of curved black and white stripes.

Over the next three decades Victor Vasarely developed his unique style of geometric abstract art, working with various materials, including silkscreen, and experimenting with textural effects, perspective, shadow and light. Through the 1950s, he defined the visual elements of what became known as Op Art. In 1964, he was presented in New York with the prestigious International Guggenheim award. Vasarely died in 1997.

If you like Op Art or admire the psychedelic aesthetic of the 1960s and '70s, Vasarely is your man. Many of his silkscreen prints are held in high esteem by modern art collectors, yet prices for his work, as of this writing, have not risen as much as one would expect.

Items to look for

☛ Vasarely prints from the 1960s and '70s cost between $1,600 and $2,400 if purchased from galleries, but bargains can be had in other venues.

Top tips

• I recently bought a Vasarely for a mere $130 at auction that I'm sure was—at that moment—worth over $800.
• If buying a print, bear in mind that the lower the edition number, the more valuable it is.
• Always try to buy an artist's-proof print. Most sought after by collectors, these are prints that were hand-signed by the artist for quality control and color correctness.

—M.H.

CARL WARREN

"If you like Op Art or admire the psychedelic aesthetic of the 1960s and '70s, Vasarely is your man."

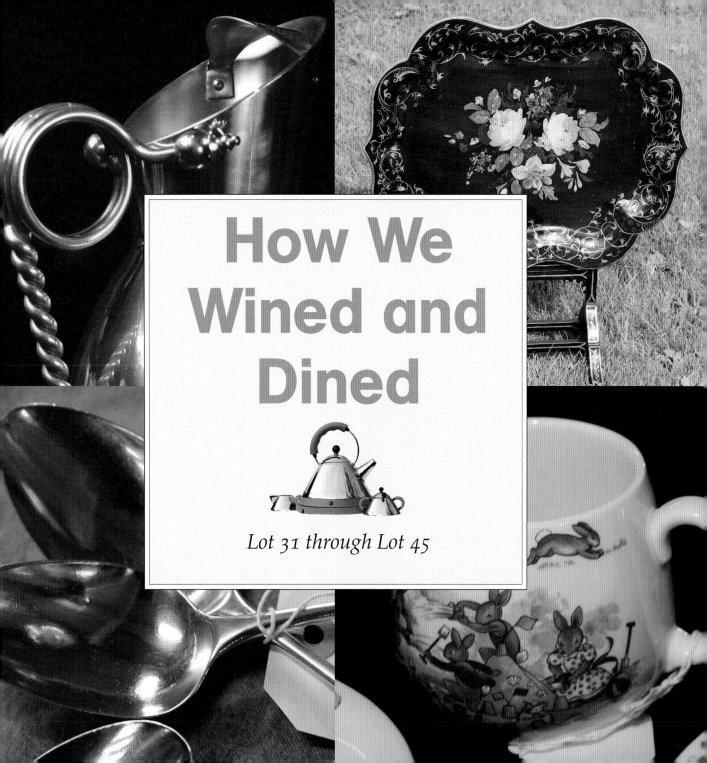

How We Wined and Dined

Lot 31 through Lot 45

Nursery Ware

ableware for babies and the preschool set has been a keepsake since the 19th century. Today, plates and cups designed for young children may more often be bought for show rather than use. Even some old examples of nursery-ware appear little used. Old small treasures are sought after; contemporary baby dishes may also hold value.

The most important American tabletop manufacturers made nursery-ware a century ago. Carnival glass producers came out with A-B-C plates, cups and bowls as far back as the 1890s. These old baby plates are hard to find and can command $200 and up.

Other collectibles originated at D. E. McNicol in Ohio, whose thick ceramic plates (1905-1920) sported nursery rhymes, animal images and Baby Bunting themes. Storybook, cartoon and, eventually, TV and movie figures—Disney figures among them—dominate nursery-ware decoration. After World War I, Redwing (this pottery firm was started in Minnesota in 1878) created

a line of Kewpie-doll decorated items. Cocksville's ceramic Raggedy Ann and Andy tableware welcomed the first wave of baby boomers. By the 1960s, the cheaper end of the market was largely Japanese-made plastics. According to Teri Rosval, veteran collector and owner of Copperton Lane Antiques in Salt Lake City, "Baby furniture stores gave away dinnerware sets with purchase of a highchair or crib."

Classicists may prefer kiddie-ware from old-line British purveyors. Art Deco items, especially those by Mabel Lucie Attwell, have enjoyed a longstanding popularity, as have the Royal Doulton "Bunnykins" pieces,

*Above: Sunbonnet Baby and Overall Boy, McNicol Pottery (pre-1915);
right: Uncle Wiggly bowl, Sebring Pottery*

designed by the English painting nun, Barbara Vernon Bailey, starting in 1934, and still produced. Another British firm, W R Midwinter, made wares featuring nursery rhymes after illustrations by William Heath Robinson.

Some who grew up in the 1970s and '80s like to collect the plastics they ate on: dishes bearing characters from Sesame Street or Curious George, for instance. And do look at today's nursery-ware. Newer characters may eventually show as good a profit as Mickey or Minnie Mouse.

Items to look for

☞ Box-top freebies (or low-cost) ware such as the 1940s Roy Rogers cup distributed by Quaker Oats, the Ovaltine Uncle Wiggly mug, the cereal bowl once offered by Wheaties.
☞ Goodies featured in a 1960s Betty Crocker catalogue—today you'll pay $15 for a plate or $35 for the Raggedy Ann and Andy dinner set.
☞ A Donald Duck divided dinner plate made by Homer Laughlin in the 1950s can fetch $80.

☞ You will pay more for items from prestigious china makers such as Wedgwood; especially worthy are pieces issued as limited editions. Very desirable are Royal Doulton pre-1950s Bunnykins figurines, some stamped Barbara Vernon on the base. Expect to pay $200-$400. Boxed figures from the 1970s and 1980s hover in the $100 range; more recent Bunnykins sells at prices in the tens of dollars.
☞ A Care Bear bowl, mug and plate set sells new for $12 online.

Top tips

• As with all china and collectible ceramics, make sure that your potential purchase is free of scratches or other damage, and bears no evidence of repair.
• Be sure to keep the original packaging when investing in contemporary nursery ware.
— M.H. & L.A.

Left: Raggedy Ann & Andy set (1941), Crooksville Pottery; below: Bunnykins mug by Barbara Vernon Bailey

COURTESY OF COPPERTONLANE

CARL WARREN

Teacups and Saucers

Collecting individual pairs of teacups and saucers is a good initiation into the world of antiques, and will give any collector a strong grasp of the styles and designs used in pottery and porcelain from the past to the present day.

Tea-drinking became fashionable in England in the first quarter of the 18th-century, and soon spread to its North American colonies, thanks to imports from China and India via the East India Company. The first teacups were more like bowls, but ladies found that they were burning their fingers on the hot sides, so by 1750 a handle affixed to the bowl had become the norm.

Many of the top 18th-century English factories, among them Worcester, Chelsea, Derby and Wedgwood, produced cups and saucers, now rare enough and desired enough to cost collectors thousands of dollars a pair. A mid-1700s gilded, Gold-Anchor marked Chelsea set with painted exotic birds has been priced at over $5,000. Yet there is no need to spend this sort of money on your collection. Instead, start with 19th-century cups and saucers which turn up in many different guises and are far more affordable. Furthermore, china teacups and saucers are a collecting area in which you can afford to be fussy, so you should never buy restored or damaged items.

CARL WARREN

Items to look for

☞ Nineteenth-century cups and saucers. Expect to pay $10-$50 for a single cup and saucer set. There is so much variety out there that you can quickly build up a collection that represents a wide range of different styles.

☞ Cups and saucers from 1910 to 1970. Look for examples of a notable designer and/or those that typify a particular era. You will usually pay anywhere from $15 to $60, depending on rarity. The typical cup and saucer of Depression glass goes for about $30. However, a cup and saucer from a relatively rare Wedgwood pattern from the 1930s might cost a hundred dollars or two.

Top tips

• When buying cup and saucer sets, always make sure the cup and saucer match perfectly. This can be done by checking the registration number or pattern number on the bottom of each item.

• Check for signs of restoration and damage, both of which will devalue an item.

—M.H.

Sugar Crushers

*S*ugar crushers make wonderfully funky cocktail stirrers, so why not get in now and invest in something that will not only impress your friends, but will likely make you a tidy profit!

*T*racing the history of the sugar crusher is far from simple. It is believed that it was invented in the 18th century, when it was impossible to buy bags of granulated sugar—one had to break a lump off a sugar loaf and place it in a drink using sugar tongs. The sugar crusher was then needed to grind the softening lumps against the inside of the cup or glass.

The prime time for the sugar crusher was definitely the mid-Victorian period. Most were made of glass, and ranged from clear rods with simple, flattened ends to more intricate crushers with elaborate ends squeezed between patterned molds. The most ornate examples are twisted like barley sugar, and are five to six inches long. Victorian sugar crushers are rarely recognized as such, as many people mistake them for cocktail stirrers. It is thus occasionally possible to buy a sugar crusher for as little as a dollar.

Items to look for

☛ Top-end, solid silver 18th-century crushers for $300-$500. Good luck finding them though, as these are extremely rare.

☛ Candy-twist, colored-glass sugar crushers. Expect to pay between $50-$100 apiece if the retailer knows what he or she is selling. If the seller thinks they are cocktail stirrers, you may need to part with no more than $10 or $20.

☛ Clear-glass 19th-century or early-20th-century sugar crushers for $1-$10.

Top tips

• Silver sugar crushers are extremely rare and they can be quite costly. Easier to find are examples in Sheffield silver plate from the late 18th century, which you often can secure for the bargain price of $30-$40.

• Most good silversmiths can re-plate a sugar crusher with little difficulty. Furthermore, because it is a small item, the cost is inexpensive. Best of all, professional re-plating is acceptable to most collectors.

—M.H.

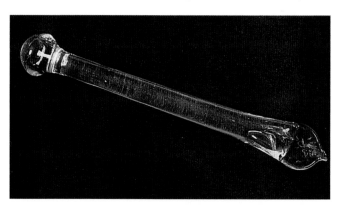

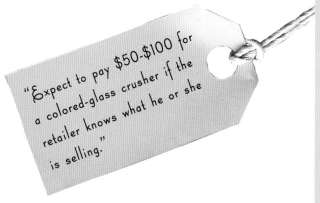

"Expect to pay $50-$100 for a colored-glass crusher if the retailer knows what he or she is selling."

Tureens

The earliest tureens date from the late-18th or early-19th century. They were made from porcelain and hand-painted, and are a class above the later, run-of-the-mill earthenware tureens.

Most tureens from the late 19th and early 20th centuries were based on earlier styles, and issue from top china makers, including Wedgwood, Meissen, Vienna and Spode. Now also popular are Masons Ironstone tureens with Chinese decoration.

There was a time when it was considered highly decadent to serve one's vegetables in a tureen with a lid that matched one's dinner service.

Unlikely as it may seem, you can buy antique porcelain tureens for $10 to $30 in junk shops today—less than the price of contemporary equivalents.

Tureens come in a huge variety of colors, patterns, shapes and sizes. There is no need to be fussy when collecting tureens and lids for your own use. A mix-and-match piece is just fine as long as the lid fits and compliments the base! But there is a tip below to assure perfect matches if that's what you prefer.

Items to look for

☛ A top-end, 19th-century hand-painted china tureen with a lid, and on its original stand, will cost between $200 and $1,000, depending on the maker, size and design.

☛ Earthenware tureens from Masons Ironstone, and Staffordshire unmarked tureens and lids. Expect to pay $100-$150.

☛ Tureens and lids from the Art Deco period right up through the 1970s can be found at almost giveaway prices. Go for strong, banded colors and minimalist design. They're underpriced at between $10 and $50.

Top tips

• A tureen with its original lid and plate-stand will be more valuable.

• Always check that the registration number or design number is marked on the underside of the lid, and bases of the bowl and the stand. This will help ensure that you have a matching set.

• Porcelain tureens from top factories like Coalport, Wedgwood and Meissen represent a good investment.

• Check for signs of restoration, as this will affect the item's price. This is quite simple to investigate: hold the item up to the light to reveal any flaws or cracks.

—M.H.

CARL WARREN

"A tureen with its original lid is more valuable."

Novelty Cruet Sets

ruet sets are small, often intricate and delicate containers for salt, pepper, mustard, oil and vinegar or other condiments. Think of any shape and style, and you can all but guarantee that a cruet set has been made to represent it. Compact and easy to display, cruet sets are most popular with collectors.

I suggest that you start your collection by concentrating on the period 1890-1910, and work your way through to 1990. This way you will build up knowledge of changing trends in cruet-making. The entry level for collectors can be as low as $4 or $5. Among the more popular pieces are those that were made by well-known china makers. Investing in top designer or dinnerware company names will always bring good returns.

Items to look for

☞ A set that represents the period in which it was made.
☞ Carlton China cruets of vegetables on a small leaf-like tray from the 1950s. Expect to pay $50-$100.
☞ Vegetable and fruit shapes have not been uncommon for salt and pepper shakers, and other condiment holders. Sets by less-well known porcelain companies can be found for considerably less, if you decide to organize a collection by theme.
☞ Cruets were also made in glass; a mid-century pressed glass container would go for a couple of dollars while an earlier multi-piece set of cut Cranberry glass could be $100.
☞ Sets of animal-shaped containers. These will cost $30-$60.
☞ Sets shaped like cartoon characters or characters from films. Expect to pay $20-$40.
☞ Sets where an individual piece looks puzzling but two or more containers placed together form an identifiable object. Known as mystery cruets, such a set goes for $15 to $75, depending on quality and number of pieces.

Top tips

• Check that each piece is well-painted and undamaged, and bears no evidence of repair. See that tops and stoppers are intact.
• With cruet sets from the 1900-1920s, ensure that the china

stand is present.
• If you're on a foreign vacation, keep an eye open for unusual cruets from your time period or on your theme. Dinnerware makers everywhere unleashed their imaginations on cruets, and you're likely to find appealing novelties throughout Europe and, to a lesser extent, elsewhere.

—M.H.

73

"The entry level for collectors can be $4 or $5."

CARL WARREN

Aluminum Serving Ware

The pride of Depression brides and war brides, aluminum tableware is, at last, enjoying a revival. This tableware was popular because it had some of the glitter of silver (and silver plate) without the tedious upkeep of polishing and certainly without the high price tag.

Aluminum was plentiful in the 1930s and very early 1940s before it was diverted to battle, adding a special patina to that still left on the domestic ware market.

Vintage aluminum objects come in many forms: handmade, hammered, spun and often also anodized (treated with a chemically-protective hard finish). Anyone interested in retro design should consider collecting prewar aluminum tableware. It's cool to the touch despite its "hot" Deco look, and it's still inexpensive.

Items to look for

☛ Russel Wright's spun aluminum vases and ice buckets are museum-worthy pieces. The silvery glow of his spun works gives them a horizontal, grainy finish that becomes part of their sleek designs. Some pieces are accented with wood, and each is stamped with his name. Wright's work covered the best suburban buffet tables. His pitchers, bowls and serving platters were nearly as important to backyard cookout parties as the charcoal grill. Expect to pay $200 to $400 for a good-condition period piece. Large punch-bowl sets bring $1000; bun warmers can be had for under $100. Reissues of his 1930 designs are currently manufactured by HK Designs exclusively for Russel Wright Studios. The new pieces are stamped with Russel Wright's block signature and the HK logo. Prices for new ware range from $80-$200.

☛ Wendell August and Arthur Amour each created good-looking, handmade, hammered-aluminum serving ware. An original August ice bucket that sold for $8 in the 1930s goes for $100 today. Arthur Amour worked for August before he broke away to design hammered pieces with animals and flowers. Some were anodized, giving the aluminum an attractive bronze or golden cast. Luckily, much of Amour's and some of August's work is still very affordable in the neighborhood of $25.

☛ Trademark Lines: Worth seeking is the Alcoa line named,

"Kensington," that included Deco cocktail shakers, platters and other giftware. Also look for Frederic Buehner's pitchers and other tableware, with twisted aluminum detail, that were stamped B.W. Buenilum. Also keep an eye out for Cellini-craft's elegant but modestly-priced serving pieces, stamped Argental. These chargers, candy dishes, pitchers and candlesticks were made to look like traditional silver pieces. Vintage pieces in all these lines go for $50-$125.

☛ High-gloss colorized aluminum items from Colorama and Heller Hostess Ware are easy finds on the Internet. They are so high kitsch. A vintage set of sherbet cups comes in a rainbow of brilliant, shiny colors, and will set you back $75 or a little bit more. New-production bowls and drinking glasses sell for $25 for a set of six. Buy and hold onto them.

A Russell Wright spun aluminum ice bucket (circa 1930)

Top tips

• Look for impressed name of the designer on the bottom.

• Aluminum is a relatively soft metal. Stay away from vintage items that are very scratched, dented or dinged.

• White hazing on a piece of aluminum ware means it was exposed to salt too long at the beach. Acid drip marks or pitting means it too long held acidic drinks (something lemony, perhaps).

• Clean dulled ware with automotive chrome cleaner to bring back the shine.

—L.A.

Left: A B.W. Buenilum pitcher (1940); below: hand forged punchbowl by Wendell August (circa 1930)

Cutting-Edge Kitchenware

During the 1980s, some architects and furniture designers expanded into kitchen and serving ware. Three whose work is collectible are Ron Arad, Philippe Starck and Michael Graves.

*P*hilippe Starck's striking designs beautifully fit into contemporary living spaces. His range is extraordinary. The French architect has put his inimitable stamp on everything from toothbrushes and doorknobs to luggage and teakettles. He is especially well known for designing select boutique hotels, including the Hudson in New York and the redesign of the Clift in San Francisco. The furniture in them, of course, is his.

Ron Arad, born in Israel, is probably best known for furniture design, including the iconic Big Easy Red chair. He has also created house-wares for several high-profile design companies, including Alessi.

Although their furniture tends to be pricey, bargains can be had at auction. For instance, a set of four Ed Archer chairs and an end table, designed by Philippe Starck for Driade from around 1986, recently went down for $2,400, hardly more than you would pay for an average grouping by someone whose name is not part of design history. It's not uncommon for early work by Starck or Arad to turn up, unnoticed, in secondhand stores.

The architect whose kitchenware probably is in most American kitchens, though, is that of Indianapolis-born Michael Graves, who has built all over the world. In the United States, he is known for his Humana headquarters building in Louisville and his Team Disney headquarters building in Burbank, as well as the Dolphin Hotel in Disneyworld. But the reason that his high-style kitchenware may be familiar is that he has designed for the populist Target chain.

For those of you who can't collect hotels, and don't have room for more furniture, it's more practical to collect small kitchenware, including items that can be bought new for relatively modest amounts of money.

Items to look for

☞ A Starck-designed flyswatter can be bought for $12. Starck's 1991 aluminum juicer retails for $79.
☞ Ron Arad did pieces for Alessi, the high-style Italian kitchenware and bar accessory retailer. His sleek cocktail shaker retails for $159. A pair of cocktail stirrers goes for $26.
☞ The top-end, solid Michael Graves tea kettle (in photo) is $149 with a whistling bird (not shown) at the end of the spout. His similar-looking stovetop teapot, designed in the mid-80s for Target, goes for $24.99 with a "spinner" rather than "birdie" whistle.
—M.H.

CARL WARREN

A Michael Graves stainless steel tea set

Papier Maché Trays & Desk Accessories

apier maché is made from paper mashed up with water and stiffeners to make a thick paste, which is then pressed and molded into various shapes. It is a lightweight material that can easily be decorated with lacquer and paint.

The technique was introduced to France from the Far East in the 17th century, and had traveled through Europe and across the Atlantic by the 1800s. By 1840, papier maché was at the height of fashion. Many mid-19th-century items were decorated by highly skilled painters and gilders.

Some superbly executed works were exported from France and from the English cities of Birmingham and Wolverhampton. The best stuff includes trays, boxes, tea caddies, desk accessories, chairs, tables, cabinets, work tables and even beds. These were fragile things, and so some users took great care of them and they remain in good condition today.

By 1860, the craft was in decline. Papier maché goods were still being made, but some were of lesser workmanship, and material too often used for construction of furniture and odds and ends was unsuitable to it.

Items to look for

☞ Top-end pieces by Jennens & Bettridge and Ryton & Walton. Expect to pay $600 to $2,400, depending on size and style.
☞ Small boxes, desk items and magazine racks from the period 1840-1860 can still be secured for $400 to $800. Two- or three-inch snuff boxes go for $50-$150.
☞ A small (under 12-inch) English tray might be found for under $100, but some larger prettily painted, gilded and lacquered mid-19th-century serving trays bring in over $1,000. A 20-by-32-inch tray-table, with painted flowers and faux bamboo legs recently went for $950. A large, finely-done English mid-19th-century Chinoiserie may fetch $1,500.

Top tips

● As papier maché is so delicate, restoration is common. Look for items having been painted black to disguise restoration.
● On furniture look for weak points like backs of legs and the seating area.
● Check for signs of retouching on the painted and gilded areas.
● Check the quality of the workmanship. If decoration looks scruffy, don't buy it..
● Some papier maché items have a still life of flowers in the center. This will greatly enhance the value.

—M.H.

CARL WARREN

Geometric Woodenware/ Treenware

Treenware is a British term dating back to the 18th century that is used to describe small decorative wooden items. Most Americans stick to the plainer term, woodenware. In these wood objects, patterns often are created by contrasting different color woods and veneers.

My specific tip for the collector is to buy geometric woodenware from the 1950s and '60s, particularly bar and kitchen items. These are easy to spot and fairly plentiful as many homeowners seem to have liked them.

Treenware was originally made by middle-European craftsmen who, working in major cities, used their wood off-cuts to make pieces that they subsequently sold off to tourists. Nineteenth and early-20th-century woodenware, even everyday objects, can sell for hundreds of dollars.

But later 20th-century treenware is more reasonable. Mid-century craftsmen took exotic woods such as ebony, walnut, yew and blonde oak and cut them into small rectangular shapes. They then glued these shapes to the exterior of the base wood to form a geometric pattern. Each piece was finished off with a lacquered brass carrying handle and a solid-turned wooden lid. There was also a high end to such wares of more expensive exotic imported woods, especially Lignum Vitae, for the wealthy. But many moderately-priced and practical kitchen storage and serving items were made for middleclass homes.

Items to look for

☞ Quirky things such as tobacco boxes, matchbox holders, letter racks and pen racks. These examples are not always easy to find, but they are affordable at $20-$30.
☞ Practical items such as ice buckets or cookie jars. Expect to pay $15-$30, but ensure that the original interior liner is intact.

☞ Carved animals. Often described as "Black Forest animals," because of the origin of the wood used, small creatures cost about $100 each, large beasts can reach up to $6,000.

Top tip

• If the item looks a bit grubby, don't let yourself be put off. This is usually just household grime or nicotine, and is easy to remove with a light soapy water mix followed by a coat of good furniture wax. Do not immerse the wood in water; rather, wipe the piece gently with a cloth.
—M.H.

CARL WARREN

Treenware ice bucket

Scandinavian Glass

*G*lass has been a key area of antique collecting for the past century. *I* am tipping Scandinavian glass from the 1960s to the '80s as the hot trend to come.

ALAN MARSHALL

*I*n Scandinavia, glassmaking pieces were blown into molds, allowing high output and consistency. Most Scandinavian styles have dramatic shapes and designs in vibrant colors. Nature and the northern landscape were important inspirations to some glassmakers, who made pieces with surfaces that remind the viewer of ice or bark. Organic asymmetric forms and optical effects were also popular and can still be found at affordable prices.

Items to look for

☛ The companies to look for are Riihimaen Lasi Oy, Holmegaard Glassworks, Kosta Boda, Orrefors, Kastrup-Holmegaard and Nuutajarvi Notsjo. Noteworthy designers are Nanni Steel, Helena Tynel, Vicke Lindstrand, Tapio Wirkkala, Timo Sarpaneva, Per Lutken, Otto Brauer and Michael Bang.

☛ Pieces signed by the artist, especially from top factories such as Kosta Boda and Orrefors. Some signed their pieces with initials and dates; others carry the full signature. Signed pieces by Vicke Lindstrand for Kosta Boda are sometimes initialed: LH. Expect to pay between $200 and $600 for good signed pieces, depending on style and pattern.

☛ Look for pieces with a minimalist look, now for $40-$100.

Top tips

• Many lesser-known Scandinavian artists signed their works. Even if the signature is unfamiliar, the fact that the piece is signed will still add value.

• Some American and English manufacturers produced pieces similar to those the Scandinavians were making. These are also worth collecting, with prices currently as cheap as $20.

• The size of a piece will not affect its value, but pieces with intricate designs or unusual shapes will generally be more valuable.

—M.H.

"Nature and northern landscape were important inspirations."

79

Iconic Mid-Century Dishware

*F*loral and *O*riental designs prevailed in dishware until modernism came to the plate with gusto in the 1930s. *If* you'd like to collect, seize upon dishware that's absolutely iconic of the era or decade in which it was introduced, or go for the work of an outstanding designer.

*A*rguably, the 20th century's most important dishware was made in the U.S.A. Back in 1936, the Homer McLaughlin China Company introduced glazed, solid-color Fiesta dishes in cobalt blue, light green and a very few other hues to brighten up the Depression. The manufacturer was an innovator in supermarket promotions to help move its product at a time when consumer cash was very scarce. One of its early colors was a bright orange with traces of uranium oxide in its mix. The color was discontinued after Uncle Sam decided that the A-bomb Manhattan project needed uranium more than Homer McLaughlin did.

In 1950, the company introduced colors, such as

"Lot 41" Photos by Carl Warren

chartreuse, yellow, and turquoise that all but sum up that decade. Fiesta-ware was discontinued in 1973 after long faltering sales, but the older examples were already collectible. In 1986, Fiesta was brought back. By 2006, it came in 34 colors, including a turquoise not quite the same as the first turquoise. Whole books have been written about collecting Fiesta. Go where many others have been if you have a good eye for color, but there's no reason to go into other fine points here.

A few years before Fiesta burst on the scene, a young English ceramics designer, Susie Cooper, who worked for the A.E. Gray pottery in her native land, had rolled up her sleeves and created a fantastic lusterware with geometric patterns for her employer. Gray knew what it had. It developed a factory mark in her honor— a steamship at full speed that incorporated the words: Designed by Susie Cooper.

In 1929, Susie struck out on her own and established the Susie Cooper Pottery, which in 1931 moved into her studio, Crown Works. There, she came up with her Cube Shape and Kestrel lines. Decades later, in 1965, Susie Cooper Productions was bought by Wedgwood, where the still-inventive designer created the popular Carnaby Daisy pattern.

No dishware designer more brilliantly exemplified the changing design concepts of the first half of the 20th century than did Clarice Cliff. With great élan, she created Art Deco motifs, such as Crocus and Lugano in her early working years, in startling contrast to her later Yo Yo vase, for example. How could one person have produced such a variety of designs?

In the drab 1930s, she brought color into the lives of ordinary people. Her work attracted a mass market then, and it still does. Clarice had launched her Bizarre line in 1928, and by 1930 she was Design Director of a pottery producing only her work. Her most collectible wares were produced between 1928 and '36: the Bizarre, Fantasque and Appliqué lines, among them.

Imaginative dishware, stylistically representative of the time, was also popping up elsewhere in the British Isles, especially in the 1950s. T.G. Green Cornishware introduced its bold Blue Domino pattern: white polka dots on a deep, royal blue background. For the same company, Colin Haxby created the Central Park line, featuring leaves in the up-to-the-moment colors of olive and brown.

Meanwhile, Woolworth's in England was selling an iconic pencil-line black on white ceramic line, designed by Enid Sweeney for Ridgway. A small plate sold for sixpence. No dish cost more than the equivalent of a quarter.

For a higher band of the market, W R Midwinter was producing a banded pattern, typical of the decade, called Sienna. The china company also offered china of a Colin Melbourne design, featuring a stylized black cat against a brown background.

At about the same time—the 1960s—that nostalgic Americans began snapping up early Fiesta-ware, their sophisticated counterparts in England started collecting early Clarice Cliff work. The 1980s and '90s produced some outstanding prices and the market remains buoyant. It is now international but there is room for new buyers to join earlier fans.

Items to look for

☞ Early (1929-30) Susie Cooper works take prime position in many collections. The Cubist and geometric designs and patterns will set you back $600-$6,000.

☞ Pieces of Cooper's Kestrel banded ware (1930s-1950s) go for between $60 and $100.

☞ A Susie Cooper cruet set in a polka-dot pattern. Expect to pay $150-$300.

☞ Susie's work for Wedgwood from 1980-1995 has, to date, been overlooked by serious collectors, but her pieces for the company will come into their own soon. At the moment, smaller pieces can cost as little as $20.

☞ Most Enid Sweeney dishes now sell for a few dollars apiece up to $20. Teapots and coffeepots go for $100 or more.

☞ Many pieces of the T.G. Central Park pattern can be bought for $3 or $4 each; almost nothing is more than $20. A Blue Domino dish is also a few dollars; pitchers go for about $60.

☞ Colin Melbourne's 1956 cat-figure dishware is more expensive. Expect to dish out between $150 and $200 when you go shopping. A coffeepot in the Sienna Series, also made by Midwinter, will set you back $65; the cup and saucer in that pattern will be offered at $45 but could be less.

☞ Minor pieces of Clarice Cliff's Crocus pattern start at $60. The Crocus cruet set is $200-$300. An entire china set is rare enough to run you into the tens of thousands of dollars.

☞ Pieces from Cliff's more elaborate patterns, like geometric designs, are prized. Expect to pay more than $1,000 for such a find.

☞ Clarice's landscape scenes are desirable; these start at about $400.

☞ The more classically Art Deco the shape, the more valuable the Clarice Cliff piece. Bonjour and Stamford are shapes to look for.

Top tips

- Many Midwinter pieces have a designer's mark on the base.
- When it comes to the work of a prolific designer, many collectors specialize in one or two patterns; others in plates, vases or creamers.
- Damaged pieces should only be restored by an expert. Amateur restoration will further devalue the item. Don't be tempted by restored pieces unless the item is rare and you may not get another chance to buy it.
- You don't have to speak English to have a cultural heritage that includes some representative mid-20th-century dishes and bowls. Top factories like Rosenthal and Royal Copenhagen had influential designers in the 1950s. Czechoslovakia was a Deco wonderland (particularly in glass) and today uses a bright palette in dishware. So does Poland. For the less usual, pick your favorite country and start researching.

—M.H.

Page 80: Jar by Susie Cooper; p. 81: dish and candle holders by Clarice Cliff; this page: dishes by Enid Sweeney (1950s) for Ridgway Pottery, which were sold in five and dime stores

Carnival Glass

If you are looking to build a collection of glass but cannot afford the likes of Tiffany, then iridescent Carnival glass may be for you.

Carnival glass came to the fore in the early 1900s on the back of the fashionable and beautiful work from the studio of Louis Comfort Tiffany. Several American factories started to spray mass-produced, press-molded colored glass with metallic salts. This produced the lovely iridescence characteristic of what we call Carnival glass.

The most popular (and therefore cheaper) colors are orange, amethyst, green and blue. Rarer hues include amber and red, with red being the rarest. Tortoiseshell-looking Carnival was also created.

Small bowls and jugs are easily affordable; large bowls and flat pieces were more difficult to make and so tend to be more valuable, fetching up to $2,000, depending on maker, color and iridescence. With the market at a relative low to midpoint, and a wide selection of glass to choose from, this could be the time to start building your own little pension fund.

Items to look for

☞ Northwood Carnival glass: Distinguished by its strong color and iridescence, most pieces have an identifiable pattern. The company was founded in Ohio by immigrant Harry Northwood, who later moved his factory to Wheeling, West Virginia. The company closed in 1925, seven years after Harry died. This molded glass will hold its value and it could rise nicely. It is marked by an "N" in a circle. You can find small pieces, such as candy dishes, for under $60. Large vases, pitchers and centerpieces can go for hundreds of dollars.

☞ Eastern inspired decoration. Most producers created patterned pieces, and Oriental designs, such as examples of the Northwood "Nippon" pattern, are particularly collectible and getting harder to find. However, you can still spot tumblers and other small items with peony or similar patterns from various producers for $25 or under. Small vases and fruit bowls are likely to be $40 to $100; larger urns, pairs of bud vases and centerpieces will run to hundreds of dollars. Desirable patterns include "Peacocks," "Persian Garden" and "Mikado."

☞ Fenton Carnival glass: Brothers Frank and John Fenton started a glassworks in 1905, and the Fenton family still runs this Williamstown, West Virginia, company. Original Fenton glassware was unmarked but later reproductions and variations of earlier styles are marked. Small vintage glass pieces start at $30, and some extravagant and well-documented antique pieces are over a $1,000.

Top tips

- Look for vibrant shades and a shimmering effect on the surface. One of the best ways to see a glass's true color is to hold it up to the light. Choose carefully, as pieces with a weak color and poor level of iridescence may not rise at all in value.
- Check for flaws in the glass by holding a piece against a strong light, or look at it with a magnifying glass.
- Look for items from the golden era of Carnival glass: between 1920 and 1930.

—M.H.

CARL WARREN

Danish Postmodern China

The Dane, Bjørn Wiinblad, was a versatile and multi-talented artist. His output included posters, book illustrations, textiles, glass, porcelain, ceramics and interior design pieces. Many works are inspired by folk tales; his style is unique. He is also known for his seasonal series.

Many people associate Scandinavian design with purity of line and simplicity, but Wiinblad patterns are delightfully busy. His fanciful work is intricately modern, sometimes combining detailed scenes drawn with many curled lines with geometric patterns. His studio and one-of-a-kind pieces are beyond many collectors' price brackets, but his small printed table linens and examples of his china are well within reach, particularly the mass-produced pieces he created for Nymolle and for Rosenthal.

Wiinblad's early works for the Nymolle factory established his penchant for elaborate ink-on-paper-looking storybook portraits and scenes. The drawings are black on pastel or white backgrounds.

He added bold beautiful colors to his manufactured china in series he created for Rosenthal, most especially in his extravagantly-detailed annual Christmas plates.

Items to look for

☛ At the end of the 1960s, Wiinblad moved from mass production to handcrafted, elaborately-illustrated pieces, which he continued to make late in his career. These will set you back between $700 to $1,200.

☛ Wiinblad's colorful Flora line done for the Rosenthal factory. Many designs are available; the vases are especially popular with collectors. Expect to pay $60-$120, although small ones can be had for less.

☛ A Nymolle pattern called Praline 1, depicting a woman with abundantly decorated hair. Expect to pay $30-$60. Pieces from other two-color Praline series include small round tiles to be used as trivets or wall-hangings, and mugs. These can be picked up for under $15; large plates are about $40.

☛ Wiinblad produced dated Christmas plates for Rosenthal from 1971 to 1982.

Top tips

• Bjørn Wiinblad died in 2006, and so prices are rising among those in the know.
• Always check that the piece is signed. Wiinblad's flamboyant signature is usually found below the manufacturer's mark.
• On printed pieces, such as tablemats, it's almost part of the design.
• Always check for damage. A gentle tap on a vessel should produce a clear sound. If a vase is faulty you will hear a dull thud instead.
• Older boxed pieces have more value if they are sold in their boxes.
• It is worth buying duplicates at a good price to increase later profit.

—M.H.

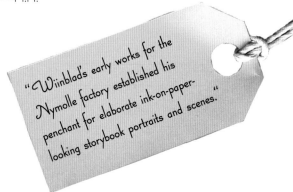

"Wiinblad's early works for the Nymolle factory established his penchant for elaborate ink-on-paper-looking storybook portraits and scenes."

Right: Bjørn Wiinblad's folkloric Linnie-line vases and trays for Rosenthal (1970s)

Rosenthal
Designed by Bjørn Wiinblad
Richard Wallo Aniko

Rosenthal
1001 Nights by Bjørn Wiinblad
Richard Wallo Aniko

CARL WARREN

Mustache Cups

The mustache cup, a superb invention by Englishman Harvey Adams, is so called because of its unique inner lip, designed to protect the user from being left with a soiled mustache.

First manufactured in 1830, the cup was originally called a "Napoleon" or a "Saucer." Napoleon, I assume, because he'd made clipped mustaches fashionable among men, especially military men. As for "saucer," it was perhaps called that because the cup's lip protected linen from drips as a saucer does.

The mustache cup became popular in the United States following the 1840 war with Mexico, and was a ready item until the 1890s. Mustache cups were made of porcelain, heavier ceramics, tin and silver-plate. Many had matching saucers, its early nickname not withstanding. Eventually, some dinnerware sets and tea services included one or more mustache cups.

Some collectors prefer French-made mustache cups while others favor those from Germany, particularly Meissen and Dresden. There are collectors who specialize in Majolica, Imari, Sunderland Lustre, Belleek, Crown Devon or Wedgwood.

Items to look for

☞ China mustache cups from the 1850s though the 1880s will be the most expensive. Expect to pay $80-$200 for a transfer pattern; $500-$4,000 for a fine hand-painted example.
☞ Late-19th-century examples by well-known factories such as Wedgwood, Worcester and Crown Derby. Expect to pay $100-$250.
☞ Left-handed mustache cups and saucers.
☞ A mustache cup and saucer with a matching lady's set. Expect to pay $120-$240 for a transfer print.

Top tips

• Make sure that the cup and saucer really are a match. Most will have the same back stamp or pattern number. Many American manufacturers had no marks but the pattern number is still carried on the base of each item.
• Remember that the quality of the painting greatly influences price.
• Early-20th-century mustache cup-and-saucer sets are the most affordable. These were normally crested with a town, or with token words. Many are unmarked.

—M.H.

CARL WARREN

Hester Bateman Silver

If you like old-fashioned luxury with a feminist touch, the silver serving ware and flatware of Hester Bateman (1708-1794) may be the treasure you seek. The earliest hallmarked pieces of this very gifted English silversmith date from when she was 52.

Hester Bateman favored spoons, but she expanded into a range of domestic silverware, including tea sets, creamers, sugar bowls and tea caddies. Among her finest pieces are crest-shaped wine labels and seals.

Hester was also a mother, and several of her descendants also became accomplished silversmiths. HB is her hallmark. However it isn't that simple because other silversmiths with the same initials also registered

CARL WARREN

those as hallmarks. Most of her work is dated; you need to be familiar with Hester Bateman's style, dates and hallmark to properly identify her work.

Items to look for

☞ Single hallmarked teaspoons in good condition. Expect to pay $60-$80 apiece.

☞ A matching set of six teaspoons (be sure to check that the hallmark dates are identical years). Expect to pay $300-$500.

☞ Medium-sized dessert spoons go for $100-$140 apiece, depending on the decoration.

☞ Sugar tongs for $120-$240.

☞ If you're willing to spend more, it is worth investing in her wine labels or other relatively large pieces of silver. You're

looking at spending anywhere between $600 and $2,400, but over her very long run, Hester Bateman has proved worth the investment.

Top tips

• Beware of forgeries. Hester Bateman silver is thin and tends to be of a lighter weight than that of many of her imitators.

• Start by acquiring lesser pieces of Bateman silver, such as her teaspoons or sugar tongs, so you can be well acquainted with her silver weights, style and hallmark before you advance to costlier items.

• Earlier Bateman spoons were hallmarked at the base of the shank near the bowl. This marking was replaced in the mid-1770s by a marking that sits at the opposite end of the shank.

—M.H.

"Hester was a mother and several of her descendents also became accomplished silver smiths. HB is her hallmark."

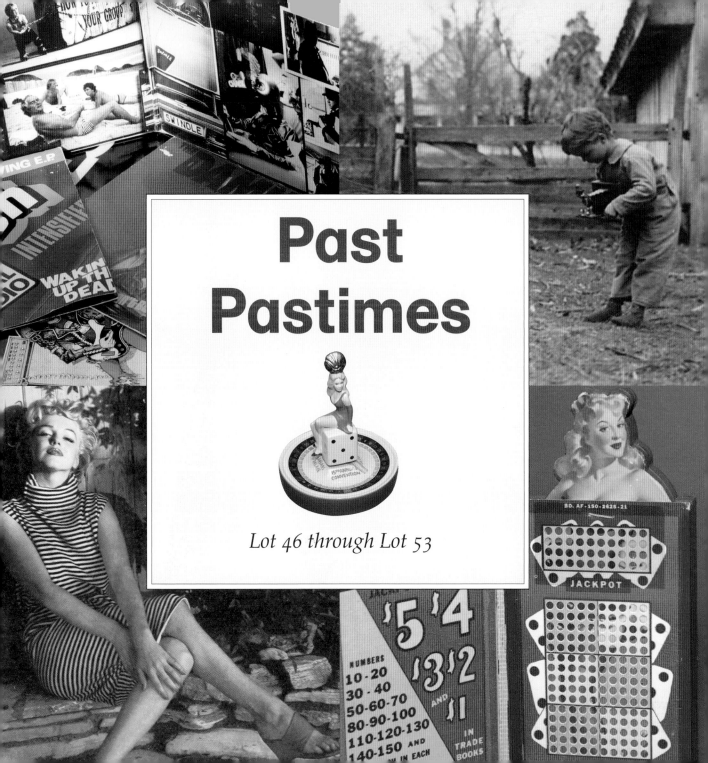

Past
Pastimes

Lot 46 through Lot 53

Pincushion Dolls

Delicate and often ornate, porcelain pincushion dolls were produced in the millions from the late 19th century to the 1950s. Since they require no special stands or cases, these little half dolls make an ideal collector's item for someone who sews, or anyone with limited space.

The pincushion doll is comprised of two halves: the top half is the torso of a lady in period dress, whether Victorian, Art Deco or mid-20th century, and the bottom half is the pincushion itself (or, on similar dolls, a skirt designed to cover a powder box or small teapot). Doll-shape porcelains that are the top halves of boxes are part of this category, too.

The base of a classic pincushion doll has four holes in it to attach the doll to the cushion. Some dolls are fully clothed, others partly clad. Occasionally, one finds a nude. Most measure between two and five inches high.

At the top end of this category are the German (some made in Dresden before World War II) models. Pincushion dolls are plentiful enough for a collector to be fussy.

Items to look for

☞ Dolls from Dresden or Meissen. Expect to pay $200-$500 for perfect condition.

☞ Art Deco dolls, especially those that are jewelry box tops. Expect to pay between $30 and $100. Both quality and finder's luck play a pricing role.

☞ You can find pretty pincushion dolls of unknown manufacture for as little as $15.

Top tips

• When checking for quality, look carefully at the doll's hands and fingers. The more realistic these are, the better the quality. This rule also applies to the quality of the painting on faces. Obviously, a lifelike face with portrait-quality features will be more valuable than a bland-looking face.

• Bring along your magnifying glass to check for evidence of damage or restoration.

• Search thoroughly for any chips or knocks to the piece, especially to the hands, nose or hair, as any damage to the piece will bring its value down.

—M.H.

CARL WARREN

"Look for dolls from Dresden or Meissen."

Movie-Star Photos

If you love the movies you might want to invest in photographs of your favorite film stars.

All sorts of memorabilia are out there for sale. Costumes, movie posters, theme sheet music, signed letters, and even props are on the auction block. In the last year or so, dealers have offered for sale such items as Bert Lahr's Cowardly Lion gloves from *The* *Wizard of Oz* ($15,000), a James Bond rocket gun "shot" by Sean Connery in *You Only Live Twice* ($5,500), and a fiberglass seven-foot-tall Batman suit of armor ($6,000). But one affordable movie collectible that is easy to find and store is a photograph.

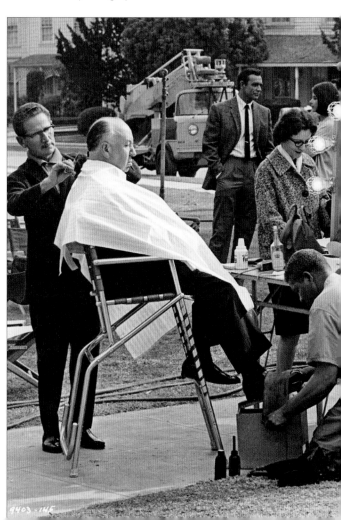

For Hollywood junkies, it's not just the quality of the photo that matters but its star power that counts. You want a photo of the biggest star in his or her greatest role. And you want it signed. When purchasing Hollywood photographs it makes solid sense to buy from a reputable dealer so you know for sure your signed photograph is an original not a mass-produced copy of a copy of a copy.

Items to look for

☛ Autographed original portraits: usually posed portraits of the film star. It depends on your taste—some collectors prefer the simple autographed picture; others find inscriptions add an aesthetic element, as in "To Christopher, thank you, Audrey Hepburn." Even if the identity of Christopher remains a mystery, you will pay about $1,700 for that portrait because

To Christopher
thank you, Audrey Hepburn

were shot in two situations. The movie studios employed photographers to take photos both on movie sets and in studios elsewhere on their lots. You could find John Wayne's *Tall in the Saddle* for $95, or a shot of the comedians in *Abbott and Costello Meet Frankenstein* for $750.

Top tips

• Black and white photos are more stable than color, but both should be kept away from sunlight and stored between sheets of acid-free paper.
—L.A.

you do know who Audrey was. And, of course, you won't recognize Valma (almost nobody would) in "Hello Valma Mauro, Charlie" but since the picture lets you know that Charlie is Chaplin, you will part with $3,500 for it. It's highly doubtful that you'll find a signed photograph of a Hollywood golden-age star for under $750.

☞ To lessen your financial exposure, collect contemporaries. Young Tom Cruise and Brad Pitt, complete with their younger signatures, fetch about $250 each.

☞ Scene Cards: Large-format, 11-by-14-inch photos used in an exterior or lobby showcase of a movie theater. A movie house usually displayed six scenes of a movie it was running. Very collectible. Tom Cruise and Rebecca Mornay in *Risky Business*, bearing both signatures: $650.

☞ Wire photographs: before computers and digital cameras, paparazzi took candid snaps of movie stars, then faxed them over telephone lines to AP or UPI news wire services, who, in turn, sent them to newspapers all over the country. What you want to purchase is the original photo (sometimes with the accompanying story or caption). A highly collectible, 8-by-10-inch black and white print will cost you $200-$300, but you can find some for $50 and some for $750. Recent asking prices include Burt Lancaster dining at the old Stork Club in New York, $150; Frank Sinatra getting out of a helicopter, $300; Clark Gable strolling down Park Avenue in Manhattan, $400, Marilyn Monroe and Joe DiMaggio on their honeymoon in Japan, $550.

☞ Original movie stills: standard, black and white 8 x 10 glossies, prepared for distribution to the entertainment press,

" For Hollywood junkies, it's not just the quality of the photo that matters but its star power that counts."

Punk Rock Memorabilia

*P*unk rock was a short-lived but magical moment in the history of popular music which sent shock waves through society and inspired a generation of fashion designers and artists.

*P*unk originated with bands like the Ramones and the New York Dolls, and then became a hit in Britain, too, ushered in by Malcolm McLaren who, with funky fashion designer Vivienne Westwood, ran the memorable London shop, Sex. In 1976, McLaren formed a band, the Sex Pistols.

Punk emphasized simple musical arrangements with confrontational lyrics. The Sex Pistols were in the face of the establishment with such songs as "Anarchy in the UK" and their own "God Save the Queen." Meanwhile, songs of The Clash, such as "Career Opportunity," underscored the grim realties of many young city dwellers.

Punk fashion loved unabashed colors and ripped materials, big tartans and stripes, studded leather jackets, mohair sweaters, black plastic skirts and bondage trousers. Body piercing and dramatic make-up complemented the look.

Items to look for

☞ Sex Pistols albums from 1976. Expect to pay up to $120. Early records and albums from the Ramones, New York Dolls, Television.

☞ Authentic early Punk posters will set you back $100-$400. The more obscure the band, the more prized the poster.

☞ Memorabilia from the above-mentioned bands as well as from the Clash, X-Ray Specs or Generation X. Stick to pre-1980 stuff.

☞ Vivienne Westwood clothing of the period commands high prices but if you can find it, you probably should buy it. Other Punk-era clothing goes for about $100 apiece.

Top tips

• Check the condition of an album cover as well as that of the record. Graphic design on the cover, especially by a well-known artist, will enhance the price.
• Beware of poster reproductions.
—M.H.

CARL WARREN

"Seek album covers from bands such as The Ramones, New York Dolls and the Sex Pistols"

Fishing Lures

The next time you're rummaging in the basement or garage, take a long, hard look at that old tackle box. Fishing lure collectors have driven through the roof the value of unused prewar lures made by well-known manufacturers. Even some 1940s to late 1960s plastic lures bring in excess of $75 each.

Antique lures (1890-1930) are hot collecting items, and the most sought after are the fly-fishing type. Of course, we're not talking about those lures with teeth marks all over the body and paint chipped off, but rather the ones the owner kept on the shelf as a back-up, or stashed in his box and forgot about. In the world of lures, condition is everything.

Generally, the most collectible lures were produced by the major companies, such as Orvis or Hardy. But don't ignore old lures made by some of the more obscure companies in business for a few years during the period 1910-1930. These lures can also bring big money to the lucky seller.

Fishing accessories from the 1940s to the '70s are also big news these days. The lure boxes, reels, trout creels, fly rods, old fishing displays from hardware or sporting goods stores and even odd gizmos are highly prized.

Items to look for

☛ Single fishing lures from 1890-1930. These sell from $50 to $150 apiece; lures from the 1930s through 1950s: $35-$50.
☛ Fishing lures from the 1960s and '70s. At the moment these are underrated by collectors, nailing their prices at between $10 and $40. If you can find good-condition examples, keep them until appreciation for them is right.

Top tips

• The more elaborate the lure, the better.
• Ask friends and family if they have any old lures or fishing accessories hidden away in the garden shed. You never know—you could get lucky.

• Sometimes old shops have old advertising displays for lures gathering dust, even lures housed in a glass-front cabinet. These displays can be worth a whopping $1,000 to $2,000.
—M.H.

"We're not talking about lures with teeth marks or chipped paint, but the ones kept on the shelf."

CARL WARREN

97

Dice

"The die is cast," said Julius Caesar, referring to his irrevocable gamble to cross the River Rubicon and invade Italy in 49 B.C. Some people like to toss "them bones" in the back room of the bar; others prefer to leave the odds to high rollers and collect the dice themselves.

"I consider myself a gourmand of dice—I will collect almost anything," claims Kevin Cook, who holds the Guinness Book record for owning the most dice in the world—21,430 to date, at a cost of about $44,000. His roll started three decades ago when he discovered an old shoebox full of old dice, including bone dice, in a Colorado Springs pawnshop.

Internet auctions and trading clubs have speeded up collectors' action. Gaming conventions attract hundreds of thousands of people and are a good source for dice collectors. Gambling tokens made out of precious metals, shells, bone, ivory, stones, wood and even teeth have been unearthed in many places. Ancient Roman dice look similar to our modern counterparts—cubes with a system of dots on their faces. But the dice we commonly see are made of plastic and even these hold value. "The value of a die or set of dice is that which the market is willing to pay. Sometimes you win and sometimes you lose," advises Cook.

Items to look for

☞ Casino dice: Most casinos sell their used dice to gambling suppliers, who resell them for $5 or less. Casino dice, from

STEVE FORTE

1950 on, are called precision dice because they are specifically cut from cellulose acetate into one-half to three-quarter inch cubes and then polished to a gloss. They have straight edges and square corners with flush pips (dots). Most casino dice have embedded logos; some have only serial numbers. Cook has seen an early-20th-century "set of celluloid nitrite dice priced at $1,000." Casino dice are collected in two categories: pairs in which each has the same logo but have different serial numbers, and pairs that have the same logo and the same serial numbers, i.e. they came from the same "stick." A stick—its contents are used in the American gambling game of "craps"—contains five dice in a foil pack; a stick can go for as little as $10.

☞ Look for dice that were part of a short run or taken out of production.

☞ There are many odd shaped dice: dragons, octagons, picture dice. Browse Q-workshop.com for glow-in-the-dark dice and stylized shapes like pyramids at $3 to $4 for a single die and about $20 for a set of seven. Rose & Pentagon makes reproductions of historic fantasy dice: dragons, "Lord and Lady dice," copies of 15th-century German dice cast in resin to simulate ivory; expect to pay $10 a pair.

☞ Gamescience and Crystal Castle are two companies who sell interesting glass and stone samples of dice made to accompany board games. Expect to pay $8 to $25. Drugstore dice are not in the collectible game.

☞ The Holy Grail of dice are Mercury Tappers or loaded dice—illegal gambling dice that have mercury in the center to

PHOTO BY STEVE FORTE

allow a dye to be set to roll to a specific outcome.

☛ Dice cups, shakers, ladders made of leather, bone, ivory or wood, all designed to drop the dice and randomize the throw without the touch of cheating fingers. If Lady Luck is with you, you might find something desirable for about $85. Otherwise, expect to pay more like $400-$800.

Top tips

• Most "ancient dice" on the market are fakes. Research before you bid.

• Store dice in a cool (64 degree F.), dry and dark space. Novelty dice made of chocolate or sugar should be placed in an appropriate container and kept in the freezer. Glass and other fragile dice must be stored in cloth bags to avoid chipping. Do not use alcohol-based cleaners.

• Mint condition increases value, original boxes are a plus.

—L.A.

PHOTO BY KEVIN COOK

Facing page bottom left: Terracotta dice from ancient Rome (circa 400 B.C.); facing page top right: "loaded dice" with magnetic pulls that draw a matching pair together; this page bottom left: a Haiden's Horn leather cone drop with bone dice (circa 1940-1950); top right: various casino game dice

99

PHOTO BY STEVE FORTE

"Gambling tokens have been made of precious metal, shell, bone, even human teeth."

Gaming Paraphernalia

Today, with the proliferation of casinos, Internet poker and other betting activities, the audience for gambling and gaming is bigger than ever. You don't have to be an ESPN poker tournament addict to play in the world of antique gaming collectibles.

I'm not a gambler, but I recently became interested in this collecting area after I joined a club of female poker players called Poker Divas. It went well with my interest in other aspects of the old Wild West.

Preserved pieces from old gambling halls tell part of the history of the Old West when card-shark cowboys, such as Wyatt Earp, were notorious gamblers as well as gunslingers. Earp's 1881 gunfight at the O.K. Corral in Tombstone, Arizona, ensured that his legend would live on in entertainment history. Today, a documented piece from an infamous town such as Tombstone or Deadwood, South Dakota, or an item from the legendary Palace in San Francisco makes a great collectible. Some old-time treasures are small: poker chips or decks of cards. Others loom large: a roulette wheel or pool table. Whatever the size, flashy provenance counts. Ride in on the coattails of Western TV series and reality-gambling shows, and place your bets on one or more of the wide variety of gambling supplies.

Items to look for

☛ In the 1880s-1890s, three firms supplied most of the nation's commercial card tables, gambling chips, game wheels, other gaming paraphernalia—cheating devices included: H.C. Evans & Co. of Chicago, Will & Finck of San Francisco, George Mason & Co., which had several plants. You will pay a higher price for these sought-after labels. Consider the premium "insurance" for your investment.

☛ Faro game sets: Faro, which resembles baccarat, was the king of card games back in the 1800s. The Will & Finck faro set, with cards and wooden case: $1,600-$3,000.

☛ Poker chips are the most abundant and cheapest gaming collectible. Clay chips go for a buck apiece; ivory chips for $35.

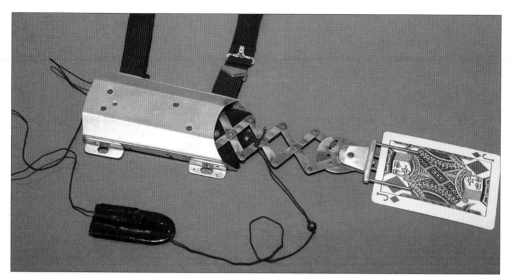

Facing page: A traveling multi-game set (1950); This page top left: A "hold-out" cheating device worn on the arm under a shirt sleeve (circa 1940); top right: a dice ladder (circa 1900); just above: Rancho Vegas casino chip

Top right: old gambling game; lower left: Paddle Wheel—a game similar to Bingo, usually played for cigars, Mills Novelty (circa 1940); bottom right: a pocket roulette wheel only 6 inches wide, H.C. Evans Co. (1930)

25¢ PER PUNCH

JACKPOT CONTAINS

$5 $4 $3 $2 AND $1

NUMBERS
10 - 20
30 - 40
50-60-70
80-90-100
110-120-130
140-150 AND

LAST PUNCH IN EACH SECTION RECEIVES ONE PUNCH IN JACKPOT

IN TRADE BOOKS

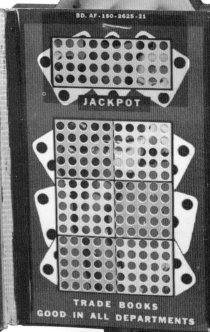

BD. AF-150-2625-21

JACKPOT

TRADE BOOKS
GOOD IN ALL DEPARTMENTS

You can pick up obsolete mid-20th-century chips from several Las Vegas hotel casinos for $3 to $20. Rarer 1940s chips from El Rancho (the first full-scale casino resort on the strip) or 1950s chips from Moulin Rouge go from $100 to $300 apiece. You'll ante up $300 to $4,500 for fully-loaded poker caddies.

☞ Old roulette wheels came plain and came fancy. Consider size and condition of both wood outer ring and painted numbers when you buy. Prices start at about $600, but a particularly beautiful wheel, with a carved oak or mahogany ring, will set you back $6,000.

☞ Miniature slot machines from the 1940s: about $600.

☞ Mahogany card boxes, 1900-1930: $90, card presses (used to store and keep cards flat), 1940s: $400-$600.

☞ Cheating devices: card markers, $300; "Hold-out machines" (contraptions designed to be worn and hidden in the shirt sleeve in order to steal cards from the table): $750.

—L.A.

Top: Card game set including press to keep cards flat and bone chips (circa 1920); below: a simple card press; bottom right: a bookie's table-wheel, 24 inches in diameter

Vernacular Photos

Simply put, vernacular photos are snapshots. They were taken by amateurs with a box camera, back in the day when that technological advance was a middle class must-have, just as a cell phone is today.

Collecting vernacular photographs is a hot memorabilia trend. Interest started rising scarcely a decade ago, and these photos are still inexpensive and fairly easy to acquire.

The camera produced documentation of everyday life: the kids on the sidewalk or lawn, the family pet, a young man caught in a handstand on the beach, and of special occasions: Thanksgiving dinner, the Christmas

"LOT 52" IMAGES ARE FROM THE COLLECTION OF TOM DELLIPREE

tree, the new car in the driveway, the prom date at the door, graduation day. These photos are much less formal than the artist's portrait or that of the studio photographer. Even photo-booth snaps of young girls making funny faces qualify as vernacular.

The informality of the spontaneous and even accidental is treasured by vernacular collectors. An overexposed, unfocused or poorly framed photo, even one in which the top of a subject's head is missing, can be worth buying. Sometimes the person taking the photo is reflected in a glass window or mirror. Some collectors favor nostalgia, others cherish uncommon qualities that stray into the absurd to become art. "The camera was such a novelty in the 1900s some people kept their mistakes," says Tom Deupree, a veteran collector. Now that most people delete their digital photography errors, old mistakes make good collections, according to Deupree.

After an outing, most families put their cameras away, but "some snap-shooters keep shooting, guided by their own eyes and hearts, prompted by light and shadow or by the look on someone's face or by a sense that something worth recording is happening in front of them. These unscripted pictures are ones we look for," wrote Morrow Jones in his book with Deupree, *The American Snapshot as Democratic Art*. "The aggregate of snapshots kept in albums, frames and shoeboxes testifies to the power of the idea that each of us has a story worth recording and preserving. These pictures stir our individual memories; they also enlarge our appreciation of our shared national experience," Jones wrote.

Items to look for

☞ A photo is worth more if it has a written message on it, or identifying material—name(s) of subject, date, location—on its back.

☞ Sepia prints. Brownie b/w 2 x 3 inch prints.
☞ Photos reflective of a special moment and era, i.e., a soldier in a World War II uniform bottle-feeding his new baby.
☞ Family photo albums. An album with a few good vernacular photos is a time machine that captures many ghosts of a family's existence.
☞ A photo with the subject holding a camera.

Top tips

• You'll pay $100 and up for vernaculars at Ephemera shows, shows that specialize in paper memorabilia: books, postcards, greeting cards, music sheets and photographs. But you can find bargains on eBay (from $25), and pay only a dollar or two at flea markets and antique malls where non-specialist

Mama

dealers may have photos heaped in baskets.

• An old snapshot doesn't have to be perfect. Pencil marks, a small edge tear, a fold line, aren't fatal.

• Stick to one subject: birthday cakes, a particular dog breed, girls with ribbons in their hair, photos where a finger covered part of the lens.

—L.A.

"The informality of the spontaneous and even accidental is treasured by vernacular collectors."

BOBBY

DETROIT
~1923~

BOBBY DIED DAY AFTER LABOR DAY AM- 1931 GONE BUT NOT FORGOTTEN

LOT 53

Trophy Mounts

The heyday of taxidermy was the late-Victorian and Edwardian periods, although there are still taxidermists justly praised for their craft.

Taxidermy involves the removal of the soft innards and bones (with the exception of the skull) of an animal, whose skin is then stuffed for display. The fat is scraped from the furry, scaly or shell-topped skin, which is preserved until it's arranged over a padded wire frame roughly shaped like the animal the skin once sheathed. The animal coat has been cleaned and probably glossed. Glass eyes are added, along with a painted plaster tongue and mouth.

Many animal facsimiles are then placed in settings designed to look natural, often with painted backgrounds. These exhibits or tableaux—such as the elaborate ones that remain at the American Museum of Natural History in New York—were museum draws in many countries.

Across the Atlantic, Englishman Walter Potter was a famous maker of whimsical scenes such as "The Death and Burial of Cock Robin," "The Guinea Pigs' Cricket Match" and "The Kittens' Wedding." That last grouping sold for £18,000 (about $35,000) in 2003.

CARL WARREN

Items to look for

☞ An exotic bird display, in its original case, painted and with a naturalistic background. Expect to pay about $100 or more for a feathered friend in good condition.
☞ Studies of groups of birds or of single mammals, $125-$200.
☞ A taxidermy exhibit with a maker's label and accompanying history of the animal, such as where it was shot or caught, by whom and when. Expect to pay anywhere from $200 to close to $10,000. Complex studies of large or many animals can go for $1,500 to near $40,000.
☞ Contemporary American Joes: Joe Meder of Iowa and Joe Coombs of Louisiana specialize in North American and African big game: deer, elk, caribou, bear, as well as smaller wild animals such as foxes and coyotes. Expect to hand over $500 for a

small mount (head and "shoulders" of an animal) or $2,800 or much more for complete large animals.
☞ Fine-feathered American work: Frank Neumeyer of Michigan and Stefan Savides of Oregon are known for their superior wild fowl, such as eagles and hawks and wild turkeys, which go from $240 to $600. Carl Osterland of New Jersey specializes in North American game. Shoulder mounts start at $375 and full life-studies will cost you $3,800.
☞ British taxidermists of yore: Look for beautiful, encased specimens of Victorian birders Joseph Cullingford or H.N. Pashley; for big game, the late 1800s and early 1900s work of Rowland Ward, and any member of the Peter Spicer menagerie.

Top tips

• Remember that dealers must be licensed to sell specimens.
• Bear in mind that fur, feathers and skin can be damaged by moths and sunlight; restoration is costly.
• It's tough to sort out reproductions. But many are of fish, typically molded from plastic.
    —M.H. & L.A.

The Best of Whatever

Lot 54 through Lot 65

American-made Damascus Knives

ollecting hand-forged knives is in its infancy in the United States. And the Damascus knife is the rising star. The technique of forging a Damascus blade, however, has been around since the Iron Age.

The process begins by alternating two different kinds of steel and welding them together. The layers of steel are then stacked, hammered into one piece, reheated and folded over and over again until the two layers become hundreds or even thousands of layers, making this steel unequaled in strength and flexibility. When the steel is cut, a pattern is revealed that looks much like the wood-grain of a fine piece of furniture. The different wood-grain-like bands can be acid-etched, polished and chemically treated to produce different colors, mosaics or even writing. It takes 60 to 100 hours to make just one knife. And it's a risky and dangerous endeavor.

The end result is a blade "tough enough to skin twenty-five hogs without having to re-sharpen, and too beautiful to carry around" says one owner. Ancient Damascus daggers could cut through armor. Today, most Damascus knives are rarely used despite their high performance abilities; they're displayed.

Since you will be investing real money, it is best to buy from bladesmiths who have been working at their craft for a long time. The beauty of the grain, down to its smallest detail, is created by the craftsmen. Knives are made to last many lifetimes, to pass from generation to generation. Knife maker Joe Kious believes "the ornate [folding] knives I make are kin to fine watches, and are collectibles of the same caliber."

You will find a wide variety of Damascus knives at auctions and shows and a few at online dealers. No

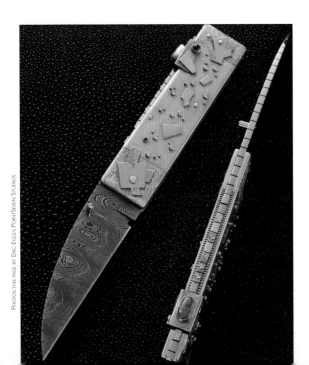

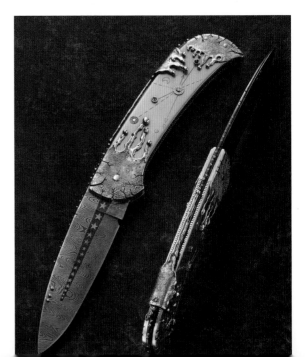

two knives are exactly alike; each is a handmade, one-of-a-kind. The works of some master bladesmiths command prices of $5,000 or more each, but don't overlook creative, high-quality knives crafted by relatively unknown artists. Judge the knife even if you don't know its maker. Splendid Damascus knives have been made many places. Below are some contemporary American artists you should know about.

Opposite page: Knives by Dellana; above: knife by Steve Schwarzer; below: blade detail from Steve Schwarzer's Hunt-scene knife

What to look for

☞ Knives made by Steve Schwarzer, who has been forging Damascus knives since 1978. Look for his novel mosaics—he is said to be an originator of this style. He's famous for producing a hunting scene, complete with flying birds, on a blade. Knives by this artist start at $3,500; a truly fabulous one will sell for $12,000 or higher.

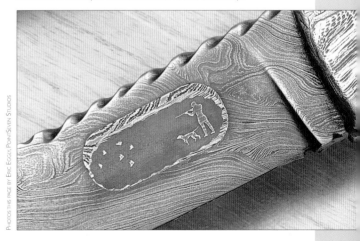

Photo courtesy of KnifeArt

Knife by Dennis Riley

☞ Look for the woman: Dellana is one of the few women in the business. Formerly a goldsmith devoted to jewelry, Dellana forges her steel blades using few power tools. She is known for creating the "Dellana Dot," a 14 karat gold dot that assists in opening and closing a folding knife. She creates wave panels on her blades; her handles are designed precious metals (gold, silver and platinum), set with diamonds and other gems. Expect to pay $7,000 and up.

☞ Cliff Parker embellishes Damascus blades with cartoon characters, such as Roadrunner. Parker specializes in small gentleman's folders, $1,300-$1,900.

☞ John W. Smith is known for both his engraving and fine finishing work with mother-of-pearl and gold inlays. His folding knives start at $3,500.

☞ Joe Kious's knives function flawlessly. He embellishes less than many others in the field, but his workmanship is strong and clean, $1,600-$4,800.

☞ Ron Frazier, Don Hanson III, Tom Ferry, Dennis Riley, Warren Osborne and Mel Pardue are not as well known as the artists I've previously mentioned, but each has a distinct style. Prices range from $400-$5,700.

Top Tips

- A good folding knife should open and close smoothly. In a top-notch folding knife, the blade will fit into its handle perfectly. For any Damascus, make sure the blade is centered on the handle.
- Pay top dollar only for "sole authorship" knives—you want a knife made by one artist from beginning to end. The artist designed the knife, forged its steel blade, made all the other knife parts and did the embellishing.
- Some solid dealers buy already-made steel Damascus for themselves and others to decorate. William Henry Knives Co., for instance, sells mixed-author knives for $500 and up. Owen Wood hires artists to engrave art nouveau women's faces on handles, which Wood then inlays with gold or mother-of-pearl. These go for about $3,000.
- Buy knives with handles made of high-end materials: rare woods, ebony, snakewood, ironwood, blood ivory wood from South Africa, sandbar staghorn from India, fossil ivory, mother-of-pearl and jade.

—L.A.

Left; knife by Dellana, below: knife by Joe Kious

ERIC EGGLY, POINTSEVEN STUDIOS

PHOTO COURTESY OF KNIFEART

Carriage Clocks

The earliest-known carriage clocks were made in *France* in the early 1850s, and the crème de la crème are those from 1870-1880, when the production and decorating techniques had been truly mastered.

The manufacture of these clocks—intended for the traveler—continued during the early years of the last century, and beyond. Small carriage clocks were part of a dressing table set. They might be used on nightstands at home or in a travel stop.

French carriage clocks, with their colored enamel, metal or porcelain dials, are among the most decorative. Some have enamel decoration throughout; these are prized by collectors. The top of the clock has a carrying handle with a small glass opening so that the escapement can be seen. The movement in most carriage clocks is spring-driven.

The name on a dial is usually not the name of the manufacturer but of the retailer, such as Tiffany. By the turn of the last century, many travel clocks came with their own cases.

Items to look for

☞ Mid-19th-century French carriage clocks with enamel decoration. Expect to pay between $2,000 and $4,000.

☞ The name of a classy and famous retailer pushes up the clock price, but many good American carriage clocks were sold by stores whose names are no longer recognized by most people. These clocks can be found for $75 to $150.

☞ English carriage clocks from the 19th century had a repeater action. Look to pay $800-$1,200. Add $100 to $250 to that if it has its original case.

☞ Late-19th-century and very early-20th-century clocks with their original cases tend to be overlooked by collectors and so make a good investment. Expect to pay $125-$300 for a good example without its case; $200 to $400 with its original case.

Top tips

• Beware of recently-introduced reproductions. Most of these are imitations of the elaborate French enameled carriage clocks.

• As ever, condition is important. Check the beveled-edged glass around the clock for chips or cracks, and do the same for the dial.

• Most travel cases were made from animal skins. Such cases can be easily restored or polished.

—M.H.

CARL WARREN

Thermometers

Many weird and wonderful thermometers were produced in the 19th century and in the first half of the 20th century, and some highly collectible samples are in existence. Shrewd collectors are snapping up the most unusual examples.

Galileo invented the thermometer in the late 16th century. It was a simple glass tube ending in a bulb; the open end was immersed in water. He noticed that when the water was heated it rose up the tube and could then be calibrated. Over the centuries, it became apparent that this invention could be used to monitor a whole range of everyday temperature events: from weather to cooking and brewing to the degree of human fever.

For collecting purposes, thermometers are usually judged by how they're encased or mounted. Some sizable thermometers sport advertising logos; these were often given to retailers to display. Many are suitable for use outdoors while others are should be reserved for interior use.

Items to look for

☞ Solid brass thermometers from the 19th century. These are cheap at between $15 and $40.
☞ Examples with elaborate cases. The more elaborate the casing, the more you should expect to pay. Those with mahogany cases and ivory dials can cost $150-$300. Thermometers in porcelain cases can be expensive. A maker's mark will further increase the price.
☞ Novelty thermometers from the 1940s to the 1960s can often be found at tag sales, church charity sales or flea markets for $20 or so.

Top tips

• Make sure the thermometer is still working. Place your thumb on the bulb at the bottom where the mercury is contained and you should see the temperature rise.
• Always try to keep your thermometer upright when transporting it in order to avoid disturbing the mercury.
• If your purchase was intended for outside use, do not be afraid to put it in your garden in the spring. You'll have a great talking point and it can be brought into the house during the cold winter months for protection.

—M.H.

CARL WARREN

Cowboy Spurs & Horse Bits

Cowboys have become an endangered species. Their spurs and their horses' bits are on auction blocks across the country. That glint of shiny steel and silver on the boot, and a fancy mouthpiece on a horse are more likely to be seen at the Rose Bowl parade than anywhere near the real range.

Wherever there were cowboys and horses, there were craftsmen who earned a living making spurs and bits at their own small blacksmith shops, scattered across the Great Plains and beyond. Boot spurs and horse bits are forged from steel; those destined for show—for rodeos and such—were then turned into small fine-leather tooled artworks with inlays of silver, gold and bronze. Some smith shops gained statewide or regional fame: these are the ones whose painstaking and stylish work you want.

Some delicate bits came from tough places. From 1900 into the 1940s, the inmates of Huntsville Prison in Texas, Colorado Territorial Prison in Canon City and Walla Walla penitentiary in Washington state forged handsome spurs. Most collectible of the hard-time spurs is the output from Colorado. By the 1920s, spurs were mass produced. Nevertheless, the handwork of cheap prison labor remained in demand.

What to look for

☞ There are two spur styles: California and Texas. California spurs are constructed of two pieces and reflect the decorative tradition of south-of-the border silversmiths, with elaborate engraving on both sides of the heel band and on the shank. Texas-style is a one-piece object, beautifully decorated only on the outside of the band. It was commonplace for a cowboy to bring a design he liked to a blacksmith and ask him to copy it. Most spurs and bits remain affordable but the best buys are going the way of the old cowhand. If you see Texas spurs or bits for $200 bring 'em in, because $500 has already become the arty asking price. And even today you might need ten times more for an exceptionally fine handcrafted souvenir of the American West.

☞ Ironically, some early western-style spurs were made back east: August Buermann from New Jersey and North & Judd from Connecticut sent mass-produced spurs to large western cattle ranches from the 1870s to 1917.

☞ The Texas work of J.O. Bass, G.A. Bischoff, and Adolf Bayers is very collectible.

☞ Phillips and Gutierrez made bits and spurs in Cheyenne, Wyoming, for just a couple of years, 1917 and 1918. Their work is relatively rare and therefore much sought.

☞ Around 1920, three Texas cow-country blacksmiths—Oscar Crockett, P.M. Kelly and J.R. McChesney each equipped his workshop with machines to produce spurs faster. Look for the stuff of any of them. McChesney later invented for cowboys the "ladies leg spur," (in photo) which gets its name from its shape. Collectors spar for this spur.

☞ The work of two top California craftsmen, G.S. Garcia and Mike Morales, is well worth the finding. You'll see the Mexican influence in the work of both.

☞ The designs of a few contemporaries warrant attention: Gene Klein, Randy Butters who's known for his swan motif, and Arizonan Steve Schmidt.

Top Tips

• Avoid buying spurs and bits that have been restored, or steel spurs whose silver decorations are not original to them.
• Spur markings are complicated and varied. Invest in a field guide to distinguish among them before making purchases.
• Buy from a reputable dealer.
—L.A.

Bakelite

The market for Bakelite objects of all sorts has been going from strength to strength over the past quarter of a century, yet there are still opportunities to pick up a bargain.

A transparent but easily colored resin created by the reaction of phenol and formaldehyde with alkaline, Bakelite was first discovered in 1872, but it was its rediscovery in 1907 by L. H. Baekeland that really brought this most durable early plastic to the fore.

Bakelite is suitable for anything from jewelry to light switches to tableware to radios. The most popular colors are mottled blue, green, cream and brown. Other forms of Bakelite are made from Vulcanite or Ebonite, both of which are made from rubber. Although all Bakelite is brittle, much of it has survived. The opportunities to collect are, therefore, considerable. Just select the area that pleases you.

Items to look for

☞ Art Deco-period radios from the 1930s. The stronger the Art Deco design, the more desirable the item. Prices go from $250-$1,500.

☞ Dressing table sets. Many were made to simulate ivory or tortoiseshell. A complete set comprised of twin candlesticks and trinket boxes with a ring stand is worth between $250 and $300. Other dressing table items include manicure sets and vanity mirrors. Beware the cheaper versions.

☞ Smoking memorabilia: Look for ashtrays, cigarette holders and cigarette cases of various shapes and designs. Because smoking is unfashionable, you can pick up such things for $10-$60.

☞ Bakelite jewelry has become trendy and expensive over the last few years, but an inexperienced seller might just mistake Bakelite for a cheaper plastic. Very narrow undecorated bangles go from $25 up. The opposite is also true: Beware of an ordinary plastic passing as vintage Bakelite.

Top tips

● Rarer colors make individual items more collectible—a mottled pink vanity set will be worth more than a plain brown one, for example.

● Bakelite is almost impossible to repair, and any damage should be reflected in the price. Hold the item up to a strong light to check for evidence of repairs and for cracks.
—M.H.

117

"Beware of an ordinary plastic passing as vintage Bakelite."

CARL WARREN

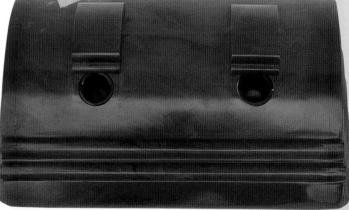

Vintage Trunks & Luggage

Trunks go back centuries. Called coffers, they were used for household storage and the exceptional event of a long journey. Smaller travel pieces did not become popular until the late 1800s.

You can find 18th- and early-19th-century hand-made wood trunks with dovetail joints, wonderful patina, and rustic hinges and locks. The military-style, brass-trimmed trunk, made from oak or costlier mahogany, remains popular. At the top end of the market are old trunks or storage chests of fragrant camphor or cedar. Even 200-year-old trunks retain the pleasant aroma.

By the end of the 19th century, travel trunks came in many sizes, from a compact 27 by 12 inch case to trunks about six feet long and two feet deep. Travel trunks from the 1900s-1930s, which are solidly made from strong Hessian burlap, bound with strips of oak in a Bentwood style, are very affordable.

Into the 1930s, the rich commissioned custom luggage sets containing suitcases of several sizes and shapes. These were made from wooden boxes and cov-ered in good leather cowhides. Typically, a set included several pieces to house accessories—a minimum of eight shoeboxes, cosmetic cases and hatboxes. The un-rich traveled with the odd leather case, or resorted to a cardboard packing case.

During the World War II, most manufacturers moved away from the high expense of leather, and the entire market changed when Samsonite discovered it could use canvas for luggage.

Items to look for

☛ Eighteenth and 19th-century trunks. Expect to pay $200-$1,200, depending on age, size, type of wood and whether the original hinges and locks are intact.

☛ Twentieth-century trunks were mass produced, so be fussy when making your choice. Expect to pay $50-$150.

☛ Top brands such as Louis Vuitton will cost a fortune (from $1,500 to $20,000) in antique shops, so look for old leather cases that can be cleaned up at garage sales, where prices range from $30 to $200.

☛ Vintage leather brief-cases and attaché cases can also be well-bought: $50-$150.

Top tips

• When buying a period piece, always check thor-oughly for restoration or replacement panels of

CARL WARREN

wood, as well as its hardware. Softer woods from the 18th and 19th centuries are susceptible to woodworm, so check thoroughly for this. If you find signs of woodworm infestation, make sure the item is treated professionally. Be aware that a new finish diminishes a trunk's collectible value.

• If you want to use a flat-topped wood or cloth trunk as a coffee table, have a protective glass top made for it.

• Stains or smells can usually be tackled by giving your luggage a good rubdown and airing in the sun for a day or two.

• Treat leather with cream leather cleaner from any shoe repair shop and apply with a soft cloth. For suede, brush gently with a suede brush to remove dirt. If the dirt seems to be embedded in the leather, consult a professional dry cleaner.

• Always follow up leather cleaning with a leather conditioner to replace the item's natural oils.

• The hinges on leather suitcases tend to rust but you can clean or retard this with a product recommended by your local hardware store.

—M.H.

CARL WARREN

Trench Art

Trench Art is the name given to objects that soldiers created in wartime from whatever was handy—usually metal, such as shell casings.

CARL WARREN

Small, highly-decorative vases and containers made from brass shell casings

Objects fashioned by POWs during the two world wars are at the heart of trench art. However, things made by former soldiers, sailors and airmen from left-over military material are sometimes included in this category. Some people might consider a metal cross in downtown St. Paul's Chapel, made of Twin Tower debris, to be the ultimate piece of trench art. Usually, the precise circumstance of the making of a particular piece of trench art is unknown, although occasional pieces are incised with the maker's name, initials, date, place or even dog-tag number or message.

The items most commonly produced on or near World War battlefields were practical ones: ashtrays, lighters, knives or letter openers. Most are crudely made. Information on them adds as much value as superior artistry does.

Most collectibles are models of tanks, military planes, naval ships, guns.

All wars yield trench art of sorts. Right now, World War I art is more highly sought than is World War II art, which makes the latter a good collectible.

(Markets are not yet well developed for art from later wars: Korea, Vietnam, the Gulf, Iraq, but eventually will be.) Antique and collectible stores with military memorabilia are one place to look, but trench art shows up at garage sales and flea markets, too.

Items to look for

☞ Ashtrays or letter openers. Expect to pay $10-$30.
☞ Lighters. Some come with ashtrays. If the craftsmanship holds up: $40-$100.
☞ Button hooks from World War I or heavy desk paperweights. These more unusual items represent a good investment. Expect to pay $30-$60.
☞ Models of ships, planes and tanks. Although these items are usually unsigned, many can be dated by the shells and materials used. Expect to pay $125-$200 for a good example.
☞ Spent bullet or mortar shells. Some are used as doorstops or even vases. At tag sales, you'll probably pay under $10, although attractive hand-hammered examples from World War II have gone for $125 in shops. I think prices will rise.

Top tips

● You really don't need any special knowledge to invest in trench art, just common sense, and brass polish to use afterwards.
● Some people find trench art morbid; this sentiment may suppress prices.
—M.H.

Beautifully chased (repoussé) trench art cups

Alarm Clocks

Some of the alarm clocks from the 1950s, '60s and '70s boasted unusual yet delightful designs, serving their purpose with a large, loud ring. I feel that these items are soon to have their day among collectors.

Wacky, attractive and colorful—I'm speaking of alarm clocks whose cases and dials were made with the sole purpose of attracting the user's attention—even when they were awake. Many alarm clocks from this period have a wind-up action; some are on stands, others were made to be hung on the wall. Well known manufacturers include Westclox, General Electric, Braun and Bulova.

☞ Alarm clocks with pendulum-style second hands. These can be had for $15-$30.

☞ Pre-1970 cartoon-decorated alarm clocks can be had for $20-$30.

☞ Plastic clocks whose decoration has a space-age theme typify the period. They're available at between $40 and $100.

☞ Tinplate alarm clocks with automatic action or unusual alarm bells from 1940-50 will cost up to $150.

Items to look for

☞ It is worth keeping an eye out for digital electric bedside alarm clocks. Manufacturers like Braun mass-produced this type of clock. They can be picked up secondhand for $10-$40.

Top Tips

• An alarm clock collection would look stunning in a show cabinet. It could also show the progression of design through three or four decades, thus becoming a historical record of alarm clocks. Given time (ha ha), such a collection will definitely rise in value.

• The maker's mark on an alarm clock is not always instantly visible. Removing the back cover will often reveal the maker.

• Rewiring older electrical clocks will not devalue them. On the contrary, rewiring them will make them safer to use.

• A clock in its original box is worth more than an example without its original packaging. —M.H.

Old alarm clocks with Disney figures can usually be had for cheap.

Phone Cards & Early Cell Phones

Telephoning has changed so much in three decades that yesterday's innovation is today's memorabilia; there are two easy routes into this: phone cards and early mobile phones. Even better, neither collectible requires much cash or space.

Collecting old phone cards may one day be in the same league as stamp collecting. The first phone card was issued in 1976; today these prepaid cards, sold in small plastic packets, are in use in 200 countries. The most unusual cards are the most sought after. Any card which commemorates an event or another moment in history necessarily is short-lived and therefore highly prized. Decide on price range and card type, and stick to collecting in this area.

The spread of cell phones threatens to annihilate phone cards, and now early cell phones are themselves collectibles. I can hold my hand up and say that I did once own the "house brick," as some of us now call the Motorola 8500x phones. I can remember my wife and I arguing over who was going to carry it. After two calls the batteries would go dead, so we always had to carry a spare battery, and airtime was almost as expensive as the phone itself had been, about £250 ($500). Ah, the heady days of 1990!

Seven years earlier, in 1983, Motorola had introduced the cell phone to Americans at a whopping $3,995. Technology has so quickly advanced that most old cell phones (both analog and digital) have been retired. Yet change is so fast that some of the collectible phones you can buy still work, albeit clumsily. However, the cell phone boom really came in the late 1990s, so I think the wisest investment is in pre-1995 models.

Items to look for

☞ Early phone cards are a great place to start a collection, as they are readily available on Internet forums. Expect to pay $4-$20 per card, irrespective of its country of origin.

☞ Any cell phone brand is fair game. The early phones cost far less today than they sold for. Today, that first Motorola, in pink or charcoal, can be tracked down for about $120, as can my old house brick.

☞ An Ericsson from the early '90s, with a flip up antenna, goes for $20-$60. A Nokia 101 can be had for under $20; the post-Matrix Nokia 7110 for $50.

Top tips

• Ways to narrow down a phone card collection include: year of issue, country of origin, holiday commemorated, face value of card. As a general rule (meaning there are exceptions), the older the card or the higher its face value, the more it's worth as a collectible.

• There are several websites set up for phone card collectors. Two good ones are: www.phonecardshop.net and www.leo-card.com.

• A photo album is good for storage/display of phone cards.

• Always check that a cell phone battery is original. If the phone has a retractable antenna, make sure this still works.

• Phones produced for famous films or events are worth keeping an eye out for.

• Seek out examples in unusual colors and simulated woods.
—M.H

ALAN MARSHALL

Glass Paperweights

Glass paperweights from early 19th-century Venice were quickly adopted and adapted by both the Americans and the French, who began manufacture of their own beautiful glass desk accessories.

The heyday of American paperweights was between 1850 and 1880. Fruit, flowers and animals were favorite subjects, and paperweights of the time came in several shapes.

Paperweights in the Murano (Murano is the traditional island of glassblowers near Venice) style typically have a thick, clear, domed glass casing that magnifies the colorful design within. The most popular interior is what the Italians call millefiori—a thousand flowers. Such a paperweight contains glass canes of many colors cut into very short sections. Also popular with collectors are sulphide paperweights, which have a small portrait enclosed in the center.

For the collector, the French factories of St Louis, Baccarat and Clichy also remain significant.

Items to look for

☞ Fancy paperweights from the New England Glass Company. These usually go for $550-$900.
☞ The Boston + Sandwich Glass Co. made light flat-crown weights. Expect to pay $500-$1000 for a floral.
☞ Nineteenth-century weights from St Louis, Baccarat or Clichy; expect to pay $400-$2,200. Some Clichy paperweights have sold for thousands of dollars more.
☞ Twentieth-century Lalique paperweights. (The "R" from the famous signature, "R. Lalique", was dropped after the artist's death in 1945). Prices range between $300 and $800.

☞ Twentieth-century millefiori paperweights from the top English glassmaker, Whitefriars. These are less common and more valuable than the company's abstract designs from the 1970s. Expect to pay $350-$800.
☞ Nineteenth and 20th-century Chinese paperweights are under-priced. High-quality clear pieces represent a good long-term investment.
☞ Pieces by Paul Ysart, a Spanish-born glassmaker who worked for Moncrieff. His early works—animals surrounded by millefiori—can sometimes be found for about $200.

Top tips

• Always check the interior of the paperweight, as the canes sometimes have a maker's mark and date on them.
• Avoid cracked or damaged paperweights—they cannot be repaired.
• Look for closely packed canes.
—M.H. & L.A.

Below: Two mid-1800s American paperweights; weight on left: made by New England Glass; floral on right by Boston & Sandwich Glass

Contemporary Silver
Specialty Pieces

*M*odern silver is a good investment area, and the acclaimed work of Australian silversmith and goldsmith Stuart Devlin, who works in London, is worth seeking.

*A*fter studying in Melbourne, and at the Royal College of Art, Devlin opened a small workshop in London in 1965. His early work was influenced by the spare Bauhaus and Scandinavian aesthetic, but he soon developed his own more romantic style—one that incorporated novelty, and sometimes intrigue or humor in his pieces. In 1982, he was granted the "Royal Warrant of Appointment as Goldsmith and Jeweler to Her Majesty the Queen."

Some of Devlin's most popular commissions have been coins, which he has now designed for over 36 countries. In addition, he has made commemorative medallions, furniture, trophies, clocks and table centerpieces as well as jewelry, all of which are collectible. He is noted for his enchanting, must-be-displayed, gilded silver eggs, and the treasure contained in each one.

A one-off Surprise Egg—its textured, molten-silver shell opens to reveal enameled butterflies on a floral bed.

Items to look for

☞ Small silver boxes with hallmark dates to 1974. Expect to pay between $1,200 and $1,800.
☞ Small trinkets such as letter openers from the late 1970s. Expect to pay between $200 and $400.

Top tip

• Try to pick up novelty Devlin items such as the Silver Clown Egg, the Silver Tortoise Egg or the Silver Kangaroo Egg. These are all limited editions, and thus are sure to rise in price.
—M.H.

"Devlin is Goldsmith and Jeweler to Her Majesty the Queen."

Space Age Memorabilia

Since most of us will never go to the moon, owning a piece of space history, whether it's a signed photo of an astronaut or a few grains of moon dust, brings us closer to a world still being explored.

Collecting space memorabilia is a growing niche market today that includes collecting spaceship parts as small as screws and bolts. Like all collectibles, even outer-space items should come with a paper trail of provenance. The Internet is full of sites selling replica patches and knickknacks for under $10. Most have never been to Houston, let alone to the moon.

Authenticity requires you to buy from a reputable dealer or auction house. Many passionate collectors find inexpensive items at the Johnson Space Center sou-

venir store in Houston, Texas, where NASA-licensed items such as limited-edition photos, medallions, coins and mission patches are sold for as little as $6. NASA also releases space equipment to the collectible market when items are no longer used or in surplus. These items may be small, but they're sold with NASA paperwork that declares their authenticity.

When the shuttle space program ends and the last launch streaks into the sky, there will be a scramble for any items that have flown on the space shuttles. Air and

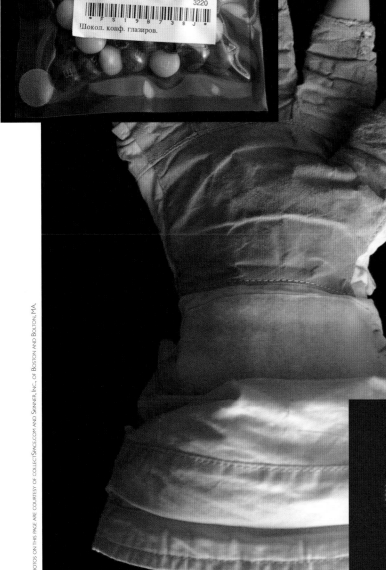

Candy Coated Chocolates 2/28/2005
3220
FS19B738J
Шокол. конф. глазиров.

SHIRRA

Space museums as well as private collectors will start bidding on space history, but you can be a step ahead of the frenzy if you start your collection now. After all, it's a bargain. An eight-inch pure-titanium gimbal-bolt costs NASA $5,000 to custom mold and test. You can buy a retired Challenger one for $250.

What to look for

☛ High flyers: "Flown items" that actually soared into outer space are worth more than those that stayed on earth. That Challenger shuttle engine bolt that costs $250—if it had never been launched into space—would be worth only $20. Moon-landing missions bring stars to the eyes of collectors. A signed photograph of all the crew members from Apollo 11 (the first mission to the moon), sold at Christies in 1999 for $10,000. Mission maps, charts,

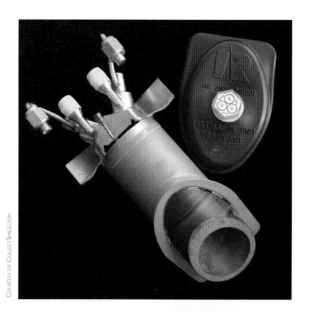

COURTESY OF COLLECTSPACE.COM

flags, and "first day covers" (envelopes and postcards stamped with the date of the mission), carried on board in an astronaut bag go for $1,000 and up. But a tile from the shuttle will cost you only $500-$750.

☛ Astronaut Autographed Photographs: Photos of those who were on pioneer flights, walked on the moon or died in mission accidents are the most valuable. Since Neil Armstrong no longer signs space mementoes, his John Hancock goes for $500 to $1,000. But you can still own signatures from famous astronauts such as John Glenn for $50 to $100. A signed photo of Buzz Aldrin's boot print on the moon from 1969 will cost $225.

☛ Mission Patches: Mass produced Johnson Space Center souvenir patches go for $5.95. Embroidered patches made for NASA personnel who worked on specific missions sell for $50 and up. Fireproof silk-screened patches, designed to be sewn onto a spacesuit, backpacks, gloves, etc., are harder to come by and sell for $250-$350.

About the Photos

p. 126: This photo was signed by Apollo 11 crew members.

p.127: Space-ready M & M's, a thermal space glove damaged during crew training. and a space-traveled glove cuff inscribed with the misspelled name of astronaut Wally Schirra.

p.128: A spare re-entry control system thruster and a Gemini floatation ball, a.k.a. "the unsinkable Molly Brown," used on March 3, 1965.

p.129: A crew arm-patch that completed the roundtrip to the Mir Space Station and an autographed Buzz Aldrin photo collage.

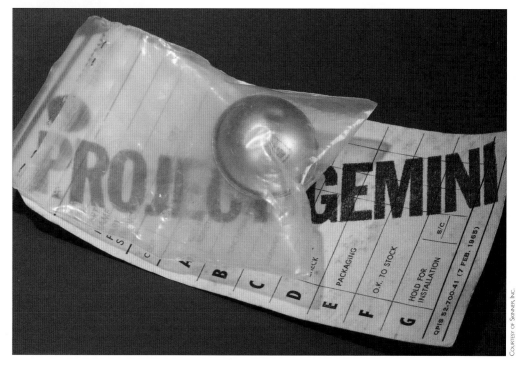

COURTESY OF SKINNER, INC.

☛ Food: Everything that is not eaten in space from scrambled eggs to cereal is either given away or sold. Believe it or not, a bag of M&Ms prepared for space travel will cost you $500. M&M's have a long history in the space program. They are not only candy but toys—astronauts play M&M hockey or Pac Man and try to eat the floating candies by throwing them in each other's mouths. According to independent appraiser Gary Piattoni, a package of toasted bread cubes signed by Buzz Aldrin and Michael Collins (Apollo 11 astronauts) was valued at $25,000.

Top Tips

• It's illegal to buy or sell moon rocks, core samples, pebbles or wreckage from shuttle accidents. They are national treasures. Moon dust can only be purchased if you are buying an artifact from outer space that is already covered in it—but you will pay dearly. A mission patch that was worn on the moon by James Irwin (Apollo 15) while he was driving around the moon in his lunar rover sold at auction for $300,000. You never know how high you can go.
—L.A.

Old
Playthings

Lot 66 through Lot 70

Penny Toys

Most toys give joy, but these little collectibles are, indeed, pennies from heaven. In the early part of the century, penny toys were sold on the street corners of America and in dime stores.

Only some penny toys actually sold for only a penny, but all were inexpensive. Penny toys are among the smallest collectibles (about three inches), are easy to display and give you a lot of punch for a little package. Noel Barrett, an "Antiques Roadshow" toy specialist and owner of Noel Barrett Antiques and Auctions Ltd., says penny toys can be found on "eBay, in auctions, at antique toy shows and can also be bought from toy dealers. These little antique toys really hold their value."

Although very early penny toys were made from heavy die-cast metals, the most highly prized today are made of tinplate. German firms manufactured these tin toys as token pieces for board games or as boxed play sets: a tin garage, a truck and a car sold together. Today, boxed sets are rare.

Penny toys of the late 1800s were made of thin sheets of steel, plated with tin and painted by hand. Examples of these often have a naiveté that qualifies them as "folk art." However, by the beginning of the 20th century, most tin toys were mass-produced, and brightly painted with offset lithography just like soda cans. Most were also embossed, adding dimension or depth to the toys.

In the early 1900s, companies in France, Spain, and Great Britain also began producing penny toys, but German-made toys predominate: tons were produced. Collectors lust for penny toys that retain their original strong colors and those that have people attached to them: a boy riding a sled, a man on a motorcycle. The more colorful and embossed

detail that's visible, the better your collectible toy: the lithographed faces of passengers looking out the bus windows, the choppy-sea base of a sailboat..

Tin penny toys remained popular until postwar plastics made them obsolete. Plastic is even cheaper than tin, and plastic toys could be made without sharp edges, a safety plus.

Items to look for

☞ Toys from prominent German manufacturers: Johann Phillip Meier, Johann Distler, Georg Fischer. Not many are signed or stamped. It is best to buy from a reputable dealer. Expect to pay $75 to $400.

☞ Look for the most brightly lithographed toys with lots of detail.

☞ Action toys that move—any vehicle with moveable wheels or an animal with a moveable part, such as an elephant with a trunk that goes up and down.

☞ Little people—the more the better. A stellar find would be a Meier double-decker bus with little passengers attached to the top deck.

Top tips

• Collect by category, such as Land Transportation: horse-drawn carriages, race cars, limousines; Seafaring: sailboats, paddle wheelers, ocean liners, gunboats; Air Travel: hot-air balloons, zeppelins, airplanes; Animals, etc.

• Mint condition, no dings, holes, or rust.

• Some toys may be missing a part, such as a wheel. Replacement parts can be bought at good antique toy shows, but it is best to look for complete examples.

—L.A.

The German dog toy was made by Johann Distler; the other two German toys in "Lot 66" are the work of Johan Phillip Meier.

Plastic Dolls

*M*any people are aware that bisque-headed dolls are worth collecting, but fewer are aware of the value of plastic dolls. *P*lastic dolls were mass produced and sold in vast numbers, which means that there are now affordable investment opportunities for the discerning collector.

*B*efore 1950, most dolls (or their heads) were made from bisque or porcelain. But by the 1950s, plastic had become the leading material.

Introduced in 1959, Barbie rules among many collectors. The very first Barbie ever made has been priced at approximately $8,000, and all pre-1970 models are valuable. A Barbie doll can easily be dated to a period by her design. Note, however, that the date you'll find on her body is a patent date, not the year she was made.

Many other doll groups are collected, including (but not limited to) Terri Lee Dolls, the beautifully dressed postwar toddlers who flourished until 1967, and who were revived a little over a decade ago; Sasha Dolls, a diverse community of young children created in the 1960s by the Swiss artist, Sasha Morganthaler; and the 18-inch tall American Girl history/character dolls, with biographical books, which originated in Wisconsin in 1986 with a trio named Kirsten, Molly and Samantha.

Items to look for

☞ Pre-1972 Barbies in their original packaging, with clothing and accessories. Expect to pay anything between $150 and $800.

☞ Most of the top doll-makers are well known to collectors, so it's worth sourcing lesser-known makers of plastic-headed dolls. Vintage nameless dolls can still be picked up unboxed from $20, boxed for $50-$200.

☞ Articulated dolls with moving parts from the 1980s and '90s. One collecting area that's bubbling is Tiny Tears, a doll that accepted water from a bottle and then wet its diaper. Expect to pay $70-$160. Dolls with similar talents exist, and can be snapped up for $40-$80, boxed.

Top tips

• Ensure the doll's hair has not been cut—it's impossible to replace or repair.
• Ensure the doll represents the period in which it was made by checking the style of the dress, hair and the overall design.
• Keep your eyes open for original dolls' clothing; these items can be valuable. Clothes must be clean and not faded.
• Any original accessories must be intact.
• The inclusion of the doll's original base, if one existed, will add to the doll's value.

—M.H.

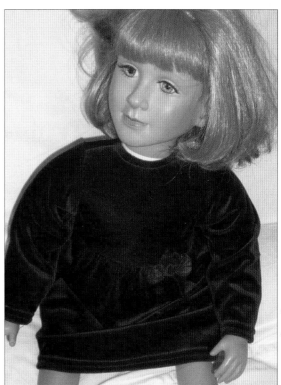

Richard Barth

133

Matchbox Cars, etc.

If you're good at dodging traffic, you may be able to sort out the intricacies of collecting metal miniature cars, busses and planes, etc. Don't venture into the traffic circle until you've done your homework.

The British call a traffic circle a "circus" with good reason. As it happens, the major manufacturers—Matchbox, Corgi, Dinky—of miniature vehicles were English, and remained based in England for decades. Now they are all owned by the American toy giant, Mattel, but the lanes separating English and American vehicle models (not to mention German and French) and old models from new ones are far from clearly marked.

The old-line English manufacturers produced some American car models. Moreover, they brought out various "collector" lines of antique cars and limited editions to enhance revenue, compete with one another and try to escape inevitable corporate consolidation.

There won't be a test on this later (the marketplace is the final exam if you go that route), but the major roads are these:

The first die-cast car company was Dinky, started by Frank Hornby in 1920. It was preeminent until it faltered in the race with Corgi (started in 1956). Dinky hung in until the end of the 1970s when Matchbox bought it.

Corgi is known for many sleek classics and famous entertainment vehicles in miniature, such as the James Bond Aston Martin DB5, and Chitty Chitty Bang Bang. By 1984, Corgi was exporting much output. Corgi also made a miniature USS Enterprise, other Star Trek vehicles and the Dukes of Hazzard Dodge Charger. Mattel took over Corgi in 1989, although miniatures continued to roll from its English assembly line.

Matchbox Cars were launched in Britain in 1952 by the Lesney company, which eventually exported its small vehicles to many places. One famous Matchbox is the miniature coronation vehicle of Elizabeth II. Matchboxes became so ubiquitous that many Americans use "Matchbox" as a generic name for all tiny metal vehicles. Matchbox manufactured an American Ford Zodiac as well as a French Citroen and a German Volkswagen. After 1980, it reissued some old Dinky cars as limited-edition models. Feeling the heat from

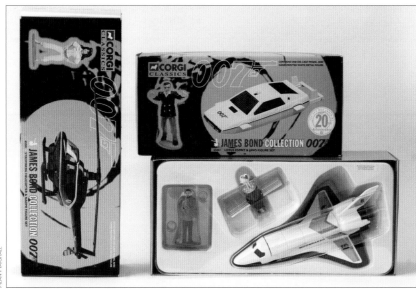

ALAN MARSHALL

Mattel's Hot Wheel series, Matchbox responded in 1991 with Superfast models and more limited-editions. One well-known Matchbox collector's item is the black Y-1 Model T Ford. Matchbox's last stands were valiant, but it eventually went into bankruptcy and then came back as part of the American toy company, Tyco, which in turn became part of Mattel. Also very collectible are mini cars produced on the European continent in the last century, particularly in Germany.

Items to look for

☞ Limited and special edition cars from the 1990s are slowly gaining a place in the collectible toy market. Toys made between 1990 and 2000 could turn out to be a particularly good investment. Expect to pay $20-$80.

☞ Schoco miniature cars from Germany are highly sought after. Even late 20th-century reproduction can go for over $100 apiece.

☞ Keep an eye open for miniatures of famous cars—and their drivers—invented by the entertainment industry, and invest in them, as well.

Top tips

• Details can be everything. For example, the first Matchbox cars had metal wheels. Then the wheels were made of plastic, first silver, then gray, then black.

• Avoid vehicles that have been repainted or repaired.

• Be sure to keep all packaging, receipts and any related ephemera in good condition. Original packaging can double value.

—M.H.

German prewar miniature cars; the vehicle with a key is a Schuco Akustico 2002, the other is a Schuco 3000

135

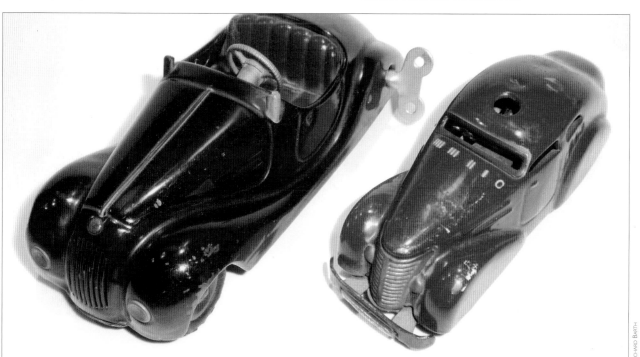

RICHARD BARTH

Beanie Babies

The brainchild of American entrepreneur Ty Warner, Beanie Babies became a worldwide phenomenon in the 1990s.

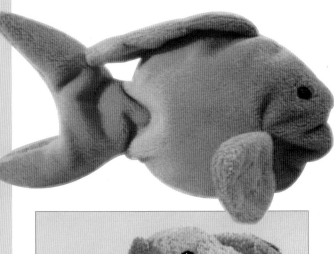

"LOT" 69 PHOTOS BY RICHARD BARTH

Though intended as children's toys, Beanie Babies were equally popular with adults as gift items, much like the Cabbage Patch Doll phenomenon of the 1980s.

The official Beanie Babies were mostly made in the shapes of animals, and most were brightly colored. Each Baby came with his or her name, birth date and a few lines of poetry on the red heart-shaped tag, usually affixed to the Baby's ear. This tag also displayed the "TY" logo. Most popular among the hundreds of different models were the Teddy Bear Beanies, but those with a penchant for the unusual could get hold of an aardvark, coypu or chameleon.

Actually, there are two types of Beanie Babies tags: the swing tag (also called the heart tag) and the tush tag. Both types have gone through many changes, now known as "generations." There are 14 generations of swing tags and 13 generations of tush tags!

Familiarize yourself with the generations and you will find it easier to secure a bargain. The rarer Beanie Babies, such as Peanut the Elephant (royal blue) or Humphrey the Camel, might be out of your price range. If so, I suggest you concentrate on Beanie Buddies instead. Based on the most popular Babies, this more affordable range was produced in 1998. The Buddies are about 40 percent larger than the Babies, and have a unique soft fabric design.

Items to look for

☞ The first nine Beanie Buddies to be produced: Beak the Kiwi Bird, Humphrey the Camel, Jake the Mallard Duck, Peanut the Elephant, Quackers the Duck, Rover the Dog, Stretch the Ostrich, Teddy the Cranberry Bear and Twigs the Giraffe. If the relative rarity is unknown by the seller, you could pick one up for $5-$20, whereas a collector would charge up to $200.

Top tips

- The tag on a Beanie Baby must be intact; without it, the value of the Baby will drop by more than 50 percent.
- Look for Beanies with heart-shaped hard plastic covers that protect their tags.

—M.H.

McDonald's Toys

When McDonald's decided to hook up with Disney to introduce a children's toy into each Happy Meal, the fast-food executives may not have realized that these toys would develop a following of adult collectors.

Since 1996, each new Disney children's film has been accompanied by theme-connected plastic toys in a Happy Meal package. Sometimes, the toy release was staged so that a new one was released each week, sending kids and their parents back to the yellow arches to fill their stomachs and their collections. Packaging matched the enclosed trinkets.

McDonald's has offered many toys other than the Disney-linked ones since Happy Meals originated three decades ago. The Disney toys are coveted but so are the toys that were included in the initial McDonald's Happy Meal, the Circus Happy Meal.

That meal cost a dollar, and came with a McDoodler stencil, a puzzle book, a McWrist wallet, an ID bracelet and McDonaldland character erasers. Even in 1979, that was a good deal.

Items to look for

☞ The most desirable toys, regardless of when each appeared, are the Automata—the toys with moving arms or nodding heads. These must be in their original polyethylene packaging in order to be categorized as an investment for the future. You should be able to pick up a packaged automaton for under $40.

☞ For other models, packaging and design determine the price. You can also consider slightly different toys that were given away in McDonald's in other countries. Unpackaged items go for $4 to $8, and less at tag sales. Expect to pay $10 to $20 for packaged toys, since these are sold by people in the know.

Top tips

• Try to stick to a budget and a theme. Collecting only the Disney characters, for example, should reap rewards one day, especially since Disney terminated its cross-promotional pact with McDonald's in 2006.

• A vast number of these toys have been thrown away, but many still do exist, so a collector can afford to be fussy.

—M.H.

CARL WARREN

Still Looking Good

Lot 71 through Lot 80

Antique Buttons

Antique buttons are fantastic items for collectors. Many are inexpensive, yet each small example is a work of art, often made by a superb craftsman.

Buttons have been made from myriad materials over the centuries. In the 16th century, they were made from gilded silver, with their faces typically molded in relief with patterns such as dragons, flowers or cupid's heads. The 17th century saw buttons made from solid brass. These were soon pronounced too heavy for use on garments, however, and by 1680 they were replaced by tin examples with brass fronts.

One bizarre law in England, which had stated that buttons had to be made from precious metals, was lifted in 1740. Pewter and silver soon became the fashion, along with brass and gilt. Steel, silver plate and iron were used from 1750-90; these buttons were often highly decorated. Very old buttons are more likely to be found in Europe than in America for obvious reasons.

The 19th century was a proud time to be a button-maker, with many manufacturers impressing their names onto their buttons. Steel was now the fashionable material, and samples were highly decorated. By 1840, button styles changed once again, with filigree, Florentine silk, glass, pearl, and tortoiseshell (now endangered) all favored by leading button-makers.

Items to look for

☛ Seventeenth- and 18th-century buttons. Expect to pay $6 to $15 for single buttons; $200-$400 for boxed sets.

☛ Late-19th- and early-20th-century buttons made from carnelian, enamel, jet, pottery, porcelain, mother-of-pearl or glass—some in millefiori patterns. Expect to pay $1 to $50, depending on the material; $100-$500 for boxed sets. Rarer and more elegant buttons are in the high end.

☛ Nineteenth-century jet buttons used on mourning garments. In England, many were produced as a mark of respect during Queen Victoria's long mourning for Prince Albert. These average $5 each.

Top tips

• Top button hunting grounds include junk shops and attic sales.
• If the buttons are in their original boxes, this will enhance their worth.
• Look for the maker's name on buttons, sometimes there is one or an insignia.

—M.H.

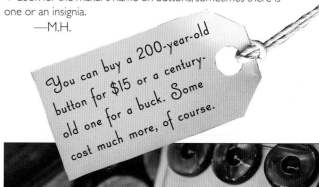

You can buy a 200-year-old button for $15 or a century-old one for a buck. Some cost much more, of course.

CARL WARREN

Compacts

Portable grooming kits for women became essentials for the postwar woman. By that time, it was socially acceptable nearly everywhere to reapply make-up in public.

Actually, though, powder compacts were first made early in the 20th century in the United States and France, both cosmetic-industry leaders. It's not uncommon in 1930s movies to see beautiful women touching up with the aid of powder from sterling silver compacts. There were also gold or silver plated compacts, ones that were chrome-plated and beautiful compacts of tortoiseshell (now endangered), mesh and Bakelite.

Compacts came in all shapes and sizes. There are handsome Art Deco compacts and jeweled ones. Some compacts were also music boxes. You can find compacts with matching cigarette cases and lighters, occasionally even attached.

Sophisticated Deco compacts are few compared to the many novelty compacts of the 1950s. By the 1960s, with cosmetic makers selling compressed powder in disposable containers, with throwaway puffs, the elegant compact that needed refilling was destined to become an artifact. Yet their beauty has revived them as collectibles for fashion-conscious collectors. Today there are many compacts on the market at "come-and-buy-me" prices, and they make wonderful presents even for someone who is not a collector (yet).

Items to look for

☞ A mother-of-pearl compact in mint condition c.1940-50. Expect to pay $120-$200.
☞ Novelty compacts from the 1950s and '60s. Expect to pay between $50 and $150, depending on decoration.
☞ Compacts created by top-of-the-line silversmiths, such as Georg Jensen, can go for up to $1,200.

Top tips

● Any compact with its original carrying case will be more desirable to a collector.
● Never wash any part of a compact, including the powder sifter or puff.
● Always make sure the hinge is in good condition and that it opens and closes easily. Any defect here will affect the price dramatically.
● Use an old toothbrush to clean powder traces from a compact.

—M.H.

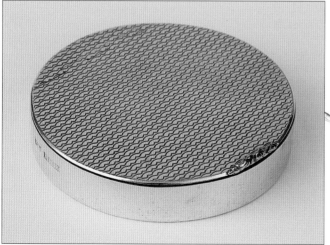

"Sophisticated Deco compacts are few compared to the many novelty compacts of the 1950s."

Carl Warren

141

Avon Perfume Bottles

In 1880, young David H. McConnell started selling books door to door in upstate New York. To entice female customers, he arranged to include a small, complimentary bottle of scent with every purchase.

Before long, he realized selling toilet water and perfume was a better business plan than peddling books. He initially named his New York venture the California Perfume Company, but changed it to Avon after the river in William Shakespeare's hometown. In 1887, he had 12 women selling 18 fragrances door to door. Other toiletry products came later.

Who can forget the company's famous catch-phrase, "Avon Calling!" used in advertising campaigns from the 1950s though the '70s, stopping when house-wives free during the day to sell or buy cosmetics became scarce. Still, the idea of a well-dressed "Avon Lady," who would bring a catalogue for a customer to browse and then return for the order, evokes in many a fragrant nostalgia.

The Avon catalogue offered many perfumes, as well as even less-expensive colognes. Avon kept its scents relatively low-priced and cheerful, and many bottles had pretty and unusual shapes. I believe that collecting the bottles will be a growing collectible area.

New novelty bottles were introduced monthly or more often, so there is a huge variety to choose among, including bottles in the shapes of dogs, cats, ballerinas, rain boots, ships and cars. Avon also made after-shave for men, and scents as well as soap for children. These bottles are collectibles, too.

Items to look for

☞ Unused bottles in their original packaging. Expect to pay $12-$40.
☞ Bottles with unused perfume but no packaging. Expect to pay $4-$20, depending on the shape of the bottle.
☞ Bottles that have been emptied are still collectible; these can be picked up at tag sales and charity shops for a dollar or two.

Top tips

• There are actually books out there on collecting Avon bottles. These can be invaluable sources of information.
• There are also websites geared specifically for Avon bottle collectors. One particularly informative website is www.find-avon.com.

—M.H.

CARL WARREN

Vintage Sunglasses

Sunglasses first appeared around 1880. But they only really became fashionable well into the next century when Hollywood stars such as Joan Crawford, Cary Grant and Humphrey Bogart were photographed in this nonchalant eyewear.

Ray-Ban was founded in 1937. During World War II, it developed a lens to improve the performance of fighter pilots. After this, Ray-Ban's "Aviator" glasses became iconic in status. Throughout the 1950s and '60s, Ray-Ban epitomized style and rebelliousness. Marlon Brando wore Ray-Bans in *The Wild One*, Peter Fonda wore them in *Easy Rider* and Tom Cruise donned them in *Top Gun*.

Wraparound sunglasses were another popular style, brought to the fore by jazz musicians of the 1950s. The 1950s and early '60s were also notable for many novelty shades with decorated plastic frames, very collectible now. With the 1960s came the wire-framed "John Lennon" glasses.

In 1961, Audrey Hepburn wore another Ray-Ban style, the oversized Wayfarer in *Breakfast at Tiffany's* catapulting them into stylish popularity. The 1980s saw the return of the Aviator and Wayfarer models, with a retro twist. Another Wayfarer moment winked on fashion runways in 2008.

Items to look for

☛ Women's novelty sunglasses from the 1950s and early '60s, with outrageous frames and sometimes floral or pierced wraparound decoration. Expect to pay $100 for an authentic pair.
☛ Ray-Bans from the 1950s and '60s. Try to source unusual shapes, but beware of fakes. Expect to pay $140-$250.
☛ Foster Grant's 1970s sunglasses. Seek out unusual shapes and designs. Expect to pay $40-$100.
☛ Bow-tie-shaped sunglasses. Original examples from the 1940s, '50s and '60s can go for $30 to $200, depending on the manufacturer.

Top tips

• Beware of scratched lenses or damaged frames; these will obviously reduce the item's value.
• Fakes are common. If possible, check against a pair you know to be genuine.
• To spot fake Ray-Bans, hold the lens up to the light and you should see a small monogram, "BL" in the corner. Don't buy them if they don't have this.
    —M.H.

143

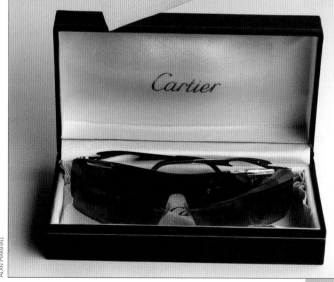

"Beware of scratched lenses."

Cartier

ALAN MARSHALL

Wristwatches

$\mathcal{T}$his is a good time to collect certain timepieces, particularly early digital watches or $\mathcal{S}$watch watches.

$\mathcal{T}$he chunky, stylish digital watches of the 1970s were the first to take advantage of electronic micro-circuitry technology. American and Swiss watchmakers were in the forefront of this revolution.

The Hamilton Watch Company of Lancaster, Pennsylvania, in 1971 introduced the Pulsar, the world's first wristwatch with no moving parts. This was the first LED (light-emitting diode) solid-state digital watch to come on the market. This quartz watch was developed by the remarkable Peter Petroff, a Bulgarian-born NASA engineer, who'd immigrated to Canada after World War II. (Hamilton is now part of Swatch.)

In 1972, the Swiss manufacturer, Longines, released its first LED model. The cost of producing the liquid crystal display (LCD) fell and, within a couple of years, Japanese-made digitals flooded the market. By the end of the decade most Swiss watchmakers had reverted to traditional watches.

The Swatch watch, launched with 12 models in March, 1983, signaled a Swiss comeback. This water-resistant, shockproof wristwatch with a bright, open face and sprightly band—in a rainbow of colors and many patterns, was offered as a fun fashion item. Several new styles were introduced annually.

The watches were almost instant must-haves, with long lines of people spilling beyond Swatch counters into the street, waiting to snag each new design. Over 2,000 models are now in circulation. The fashion brouhaha long ago died down, but for collectors, Swatches are not disposable chic.

With the growing enthusiasm for all things 1970s, early digitals are becoming hotter, and the market for Swatch watches of the 1980s and 1990s is reheating nicely.

Items to look for

☛ Pulsar Sport Timer LCD wristwatch on an original black plastic strap. Expect to pay $200 for a good example.

☛ Casio 505 Data Bank LCD wristwatch on a steel bracelet.

☛ Synchronar 2100 solar-powered divers' watch. Top-of-the-line stainless steel strap bracelet with LED readout. This watch, designed by Roger Riehl, has a double solar-panel fitting at the top that could power the watch for up to a year: over $2,000.

☛ Very early Swatch watches and the limited-edition models go for up to $500. Unusual face shapes such as an elongated "s" are very collectible at prices ranging from $100 to $250.

CARL WARREN

CARL WARREN

Top tips

• Check that all of the watch's functions are in good working order, and that there are no battery leakages, which will ruin the movement. Replace or remove watch batteries as soon as they run out.

• Always try to buy watches with original papers, labels and packaging.

• You can sometimes buy collectible watches at very good prices at vintage clothing shops.

• Note pre-Christmas ads for new limited-edition Swatch watches, especially numbered editions.

—M.H.

"The chunky digital watches of the 1970s were the first to take advantage of electronic micro-circuitry technology."

Gucci Handbags

The first Gucci handbag was crafted in a little shop in Florence nearly three-quarters of a century ago. It has been a symbol of sophistication and extravagance ever since.

Guccio Gucci developed a taste for elegance as a young man while working in London's expensive Savoy Hotel as an elevator operator. The son of a Florentine craftsman, he spent his early years between Paris and London, and it was from these worldly surroundings that he gained his sense of cosmopolitan style.

In the early 1920s, Guccio returned to Florence to open a leather goods shop, which started out selling high-grades luggage and saddles made to his high-standards specifications. His high-quality craftsmanship, particularly as expressed in equestrian accessories, gained him an influential following.

In the mid '30s, meticulously sewn handbags were added to the wares.

Within two decades, Gucci became an internationally known name, and a Gucci store was opened in New York. The store concentrated on what we now think of as the classic Gucci accessories: the handbag with bamboo handles, the moccasin shoe with the distinctive Gucci snaffle bit; the foulards; the belt clasps; the ties.

In the 1960s, Gucci started opening stores in many cities all over the world, and the brand exploded. The little handbag that has long been a status symbol for the cognoscenti was coveted on almost every continent..

Items to look for

☞ The resale value of a vintage Gucci handbag holds up, but it's difficult to pinpoint prices, which depend on era, pocketbook model and condition. Your research really must consist of comparison shopping (i.e., looking carefully) until you're ready to pounce.

☞ Do not be afraid to collect newer styles. Gucci sophistication and workmanship continue to impress.

Top tips

- Beware of fakes—they are absolutely everywhere! You must get to know what you are looking for, and what you are looking at.
  - Ask your friends and family if they own any Gucci items. You never know what someone else no longer uses or wants.

—M.H.

"The resale value of a vintage Gucci handbag holds up."

ALAN MARSHALL

Crocodile & Snakeskin Accessories

International regulations governing the uses or importation of animal skins mean that brand-new accessories—from lanyards to shoes—made of certain skins may be either illegal or attainable only at great price.

But the vintage alligator, crocodile or snakeskin purse, wallet, passport folder or other accessory can be found, although some are too expensive to be collected. In my opinion, items dating from the 1900s to the '40s present the best chance for bagging a bargain. And because goods made from such skins often fell into the luxury category, these older items tend to be excellently made.

The quality of a vintage item perforce comes down to the condition of the skin, so be sure to scrutinize this carefully. The finest alligator or crocodile goods were made from the skin on the underbelly of the animal, which has a distinctive, symmetrical pattern. Don't go shopping until you're familiar with the pattern you want to buy.

Items to look for

☞ Small alligator, crocodile or snakeskin wallets. Expect to pay $40-100.
☞ Alligator, crocodile or snakeskin suitcases. Expect to pay $800-$1,000.
☞ Ladies' handbags. At charity or secondhand clothing shops, they occasionally are spotted for as little as $30, while specialty retailers may charge up to $200.
☞ Small picture frames or framed mirrors: $30-$100.
☞ Crocodile cigarette cases or cigar boxes. Expect to pay $20-$200, depending on size and quality.

Top tips

• Always check for evidence of restoration, and remember that the interior of any item is as important as the exterior.
• Keep your animal-skin items clean. To do so, first remove all the dust and dirt with a damp soft cloth. Stuff a handbag or other pouch with tissue paper until it has resumed its crafted shape. Next, rub in furniture polish with a very soft cloth (never a brush). Continue rubbing until the item looks as if it were new.
• If the skin is very dry, do not use oils or shoe creams, as this will cause the scales to peel off. Instead, gradually hydrate the skin using a thin coat of solid shoe polish (one which matches the skin color or is neutral), and rub in with a soft cloth. Wait for the polish to dry, and then buff the skin.

—M.H.

147

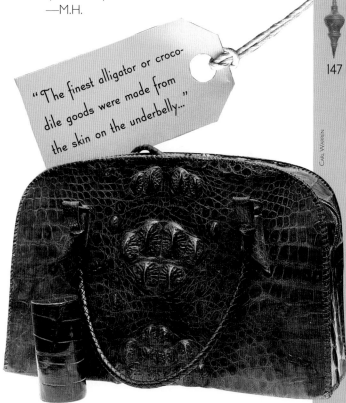

"The finest alligator or crocodile goods were made from the skin on the underbelly..."

CARL WARREN

Vesta Cases/Match Safes

Who would think that small British match boxes, produced almost one hundred and fifty years ago, would end up around the necks of fashionable American women?

148

Not all chic women are familiar with this new type of collectible "jewelry." A collector will still find a wide variety of designs and prices for these wonderful little boxes.

Vesta, the Roman Goddess of the hearth, gave her name to these silver matchboxes. Matches were called vestas until the 20th century. Since matches were obviously flammable, they had to be transported safely and kept dry. When a man went to light his pipe or cigar he pulled a double chain out of his waistcoat pocket—his pocket watch dangled on one end and his "vesta" case on the other. The small boxes were commonplace from the 1860s forward, until the lighter replaced many of them in the 1920s. "Vesta," by the way, is an Anglicism, adopted here by men of fashion, although down-home Americans referred to the box as a "match safe." Gorham produced some highly collectible, sterling silver match safes.

Items to look for

☛ A high-quality case has a "jump-link" to attach it to its chain, known as the "Albert chain," in honor of Queen Victoria's husband; a lid that springs open to one side; a steel strike soldered to the bottom of the case.

☛ Although most stylish cases were made of silver, they can also be found in gold, brass or copper, and late ones were even made in jade or Bakelite. Some cases are plain, but most have decorative motifs; many were engraved with the owner's initials. You will pay handsomely for cases set with precious stones. Also pricey is a vesta case depicting the head of Queen Victoria, made to

Boar-shaped vesta case by Thomas Johnson (1885) at left: detail showing the "strike" plate at the bottom of the case.

Left and below: Sterling vesta case by Thomas Hayes, Birmingham, England (1897); Bottom right: Silver and enamel case showing dog by George Unite, London (1893).

commemorate her Diamond Jubilee. Look for enameled cases with sporting or gambling motifs, or novelty cases in animal shapes.

☞ The majority of English vesta cases were made in London, Birmingham or Chester. British names include: Joseph Gloster, Deakin & Francis, C. Saunders & F. Shepherd, and A & J Zimmerman. Good enamels came from Sampson Mordan & Co. For English sterling expect to pay $250 to as much as $4,500 for a good, jewel-adorned case. However, on eBay you'll see prices well under $200.

☞ American makers were concentrated in the northeast: New York, New Jersey and Massachusetts. Worthy silversmiths include: Gorham, F.S. Gilbert, William Kerr, Unger Brothers, Battin & Co. and Carter & Howe. Most American cases sell in the $50-$500 range, although enamel scenes will cost you $600-$1,000 or more.

☞ Companies in the U.S. gave away match safes to promote products, from banks to beers. A case intended as a tiny billboard was made of celluloid and printed in color. Touristy shops around the country sold safety boxes, promoting the wonder of a resort or other site, for under a dollar. Today, you can pick up these advertisers for $10 or $20 apiece.

Top Tips

• Get to know and seek legible hallmarks on English sterling, which not only guarantee the silver (a full-lion profile), but also can reveal the maker, city and date of manufacture. Not all American boxes have markings.

• Avoid buying silver pieces with dented corners, split seams, damaged hinges, lids that don't stay closed, or marred inscriptions or initials.

• Flee from the fakes. Some are vintage boxes that have been recently enameled with nudes or sport scenes. You can sometimes spot a fake by close examination or testing it with a coin. If the surface is very slick and a coin slides off, it's a reproduction.

—L.A.

Facing page top row, l. to r. American vesta case makers: William Kerr, J.E. Mergott, William Kerr, George Shiebler, Unger Bros., Whitehead & Hoag, Gorham

PHOTO BY GEORGE SFERALOU

Taxco Silver Jewelry

In the hills between Mexico City and Acapulco is a village called Taxco, rich for centuries as the site of silver mines—some producing since before the Conquistadors.

By the end of the 16th century, silver from Taxco had spread across Europe, and Taxco became the silver capital of the world. By the 20th century, Mexican artists were looking to their pre-Columbian roots for inspiration from folk art. Much Taxco work reinterprets themes from ancient Mexican culture. The vibrant crafts community in Taxco attracted artists of many kinds from America and beyond. Three decades into the last century, the Taxco Arts and Crafts movement began to flourish.

During the 1930s and '40s, silver jewelry of extraordinary quality was produced in small workshops. Taxco jewelers mixed Mexican motifs with contemporary design elements. Today, the work of the best of those artists, and a few later ones, is highly collectible, commanding high prices. There are 16,000 shops that sell silver in Taxco today—much of it mediocre, but the best of Taxco School silver is worth its weight in gold.

Items to look for

☞ Frederick W. Davis: This American designer, who worked in Mexico in the '20s and '30s, favored indigenous stones, such as amethyst and black obsidian, in his silver bracelets, necklaces and other jewelry. Expect to pay $1,000 for a pin or brooch; $2,000 and up for a necklace or bracelet.

☞ William Spratling is sometimes called "the Father of Taxco silver," and was the most important mid-century Taxco silversmith. He was an American professor of Architecture who went to Taxco in 1931 to study its architectural legacy, and stayed. Spratling's work, like Davis's, uses local gemstones, and is also notable for pieces combining high-quality silver and rosewood. Spratling's early work relies heavily on pre-Columbian imagery; later, he moved into more modern design. In his small workshop, he trained talented artisans who eventually became well known and set up shops of their own. Most Spratling pieces are in the "untouchable" range because they are so rare now. If you're deft and lucky, you may be able to find a brooch for $1,000—but his museum-quality jewelry fetches about $30,000 apiece at auction.

☞ Hector Aguilar: His highly sought-after ranchero designs have few stones. Aguilar was once Spratling's shop manager. Expect to pay $600 for a pair of earrings and $2,500 or more for a bracelet.

☞ Antonio Pineda: He worked for Spratling in the 1940s, and then became known in his own right as a

At left: Amethyst bracelet by Frederick W. Davis; facing page top: on left, mosaic enamel by Margot de Taxco; on right: bracelet by Hector Aguilar; bottom left, sunburst bracelet by William Spratling.

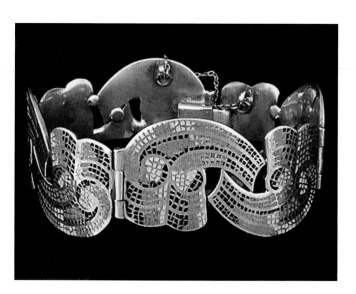

modernist, whose bold heavy-silver pieces incorporated topaz, moonstones and/or other semi-precious stones. Expect to pay $1,800 to $2,400 or more for a Pineda.

☛ Los Castillo: This Taxco silver shop was established by four silversmith brothers in 1939, who employed innovative techniques to marry copper, steel, brass and silver in their jewelry,

which also echoed pre-Columbian themes in their inlaid stonework. Expect to pay $200 for a relatively simple brooch but a few thousand dollars for a more elaborate work.

☛ Margot de Taxco: Born Margot van Voorhies Carr, she married and divorced a Castillo brother (Antonio) before opening her own shop in 1948. Known for her combination of styles that create a sense of motion in silver, copper or enamel. Her works combine traditional Mexican style with Art Nouveau, Art Deco or Egyptian revival motifs. Expect to pay $600 to $800 for a simple silver bracelet but up to $10,000 for her enamel work.

☛ Sigi Pineda: worked for Margot de Taxco before going out on his own in the 1950s. Mid-century Scandinavian and American influences are reflected in his clean surfaces with overlapping planes of silver. Active at the age of 80, he remains a top-of-the-line modernist designer. You'll pay $400-$500 for a bracelet, $200-$300 for a pin.

☛ A notable mid-century trio of designers: Look for Salvador Teran's jewelry, featuring overlapping planes of silver against black backgrounds. Teran worked for Spratling and then for his Castillo cousins. His pieces can be pricey at $1,500-$2,500. Enrique Ledesma's necklaces, which show off exquisite stones, are prizes at $600-$2,000. Felipe Martinez's sculpted silver pieces are stamped Piedra Y Plata, the name of the shop he founded to sell his work. Since he only produced for a few years, when a piece comes to market, it fetches $1,000-$2,000.

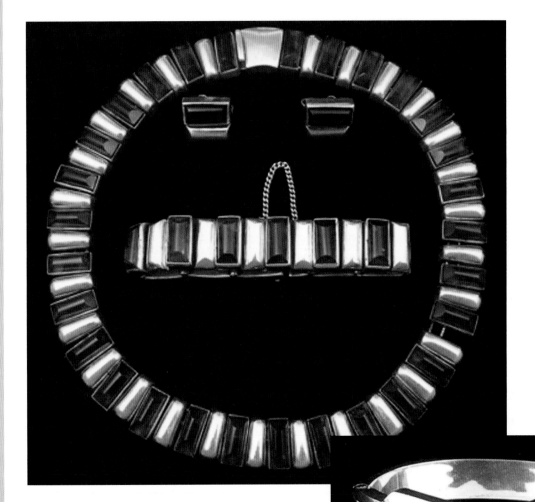

Top Tips

• Look for hallmarked pieces, particularly the Eagle stamp that the Mexican government authorizes to denote the high silver content also known as 925. Eagle-stamped pieces from 1948-1970 are worth more than the pieces that are only initialed and numbered. Other silver hallmarks were also in play. Consult a book on Taxco hallmarks before buying.

• Taxco jewelry should be treated as fine silver and kept in a soft sack, away from humidity to avoid oxidation.

—L.A.

Facing page: Amethyst and silver set and the bracelet at bottom by Antonio Pineda; This page, below left: open silver cuff bracelet by Los Castillos: at right: tulip amethyst necklace by William Spratling; bottom right: earrings and bracelet set with raw emeralds by Salvador Teran.

"LOT 79" PHOTOS, COURTESY OF MAESTROSDETAXCO.COM

Mid-Century Costume Jewelry

In the age of "bling," costume jewelry has really found its place again. Best of all, vintage affordable and fabulous fakes are everywhere: flea markets, tag sales, secondhand clothing stores, fundraising fairs, antique shops, small auction houses.

Until recently, only definitively-designed prewar costume jewelry, mostly Deco, was collectible, but the time has come to take a closer look at other and later types of pieces.

A few important American costume-jewelry makers have been in business for quite some time. Many women who care about accessories know their names, and I believe it's worth parting with that little bit extra for the bonus of a named product. Notable American designers include Napier, Trifari, Joseff of Hollywood, and Miriam Haskell, as well as the pricier Kenneth J. Lane.

Costume jewelry designed by the top French clothing designers deserves your attention, most especially that of Coco Chanel and Christian Dior. However, you may need to be a sleuth to find this at a reasonable price. At a recent New York antiques show, entitled "Modernism," a dealer was asking thousands of dollars for a heavy and elaborate multi-strand Chanel necklace.

Modern Scandinavian silver jewelry can also be worthwhile if we can allow silver into the costume category. Georg Jensen pieces certainly represent the high end here. Look for the number 800 on Scandinavian or Continental silver to assure it is the equivalent of sterling. Also, one cannot ignore Swarovski crystal-bead adornments.

Items to look for

☛ Many single pieces of costume jewelry fall between $5 and $20.

☛ Trays or boxes of costume jewelry at auction usually go for an amount related to the number of pieces in the lot, with the usual range being between 50 cents and $3 an item.

☛ Pieces by designers such as Dior, Chanel or Kenneth J. Lane (whom Jackie Kennedy is said to have patronized) easily fetch in the neighborhood of $100 or more each.

Top tips

• Look for a jewelry style or theme that appeals to you and concentrate on finding pieces in this style. For example, many people collect insect shapes such as butterflies and bees because they are timeless.

• Quality is important. Make sure you are armed with a magnifying glass to check that the setting is in good order and that no stones or pieces of glass are missing.

—M.H.

CARL WARREN

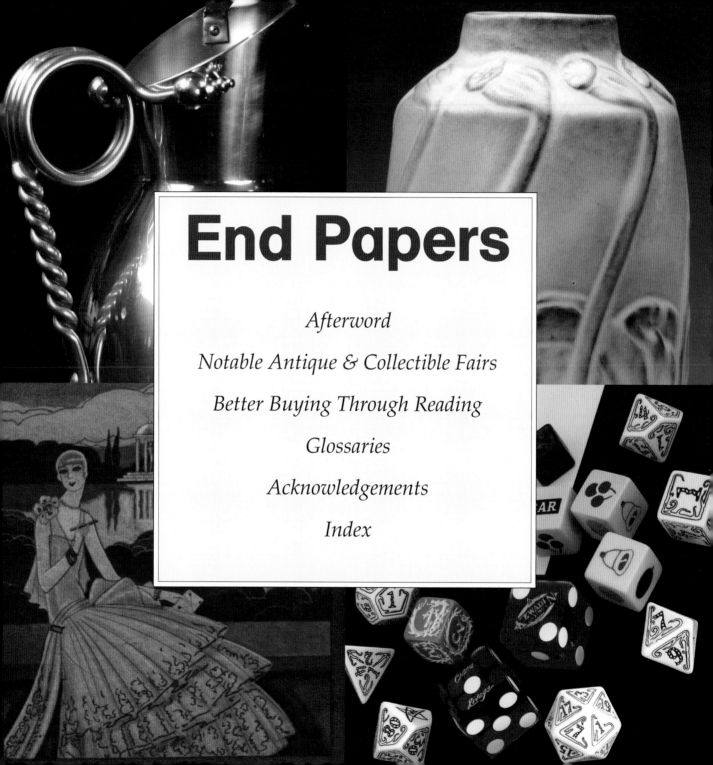

End Papers

Afterword

We have all watched "Antiques Roadshow," and love it when a casual $20 flea-market purchase, upon examination, turns out to be a museum-quality vase or chair. Such accidental finds are rare but still possible.

In 1991, a woman truck driver from San Bernadino, California, named Teri Horton, went into a local thrift shop to look for a gift to cheer up an out-of-sorts friend. She found a large painting with bright drips of paint and bought it for $5, after bargaining with the shop owner who'd wanted $8. The intended recipient disliked the painting which, in any case, was too large for the wall of her trailer. So Teri Horton took back her $5 gift and put it in her own yard sale. An art teacher from a local college saw it and told Horton, "This may be a Jackson Pollack," to which Teri replied, in her vernacular, "Who the #$&% is Jackson Pollock?"

That response became the title of a 2006 documentary made by former "60 Minutes" producers. The film follows Teri Horton's attempt to authenticate the painting. In the documentary, its owner confides that before her tag sale she'd considered throwing darts at her "joke painting." Instead, Horton hired experts, art forensic scientists, to match fingerprints, techniques and color chips to prove the provenance of her "Pollack." So far, important but possibly class-conscious art critics have refused to authenticate her painting as the work of the man many believe to be America's greatest abstract expressionist. Not long ago, an undisputed Jackson Pollack sold at Sotheby's for $140 million. Teri turned down a $2 million offer for the painting she owns. Perhaps she should've taken it—not a bad return on her $5 investment.

Moral of the story: Don't pass up your neighbor's yard sale or the local thrift shop. You never know what you'll find. Remember, also, that because your grandmother had something she considered "junk" in her attic doesn't mean it's not valuable.

I browse like a detective. If you're reading this book, chances are that you, like me, find searching fun. On weekends I can't think of anything I'd rather do than go antiquing. I confess to being a perpetual shopper, addicted to the pursuit of finding "something" for practically nothing. I prefer to purchase items I can use or wear. I drink from the teacups, place flowers in the vases and wear my vintage jewels.

Glenn Eicher once wrote in *The New Yorker* that the secret behind his long and successful marriage had been weekend antiquing, a passion he and his wife share. Describing the thrill of walking into an antique store, he wrote of "that first moment so pregnant with possibility, when you exchange the tiresome sunlight and fresh air for the musky, dark, crowded aisles where pleasure awaits. Your eyes adjust and you see the riches laid out before you."

The collector also seeks a journey back in time—a perfume bottle, a poster, a ceramic bowl that reminds us of an America largely built by immigrants who brought their treasures with them. The floorboards may creak under our feet as we travel down the aisles of antique shops, but our hearts are keeping a steady beat in anticipation of a find, a bargain—yet just as important, a special something that preserves the past and makes us relive history, something that sparks that twinge of nostalgia.

In his 1993 book on the psychology of collecting, Werner Muensterberger wrote that obsessive collecting derives from "deprivation or loss or vulnerability and a subsequent longing for substitutes." To fill that void, some collectors become packrats, scooping up and hanging onto everything they see in their collecting category. Others limit their hunt by two of Michael Hogben's fail-safe rules: condition and rarity. Such seekers are willing to exchange lesser treasures for better samples.

Then there are people with large amounts of disposable income who hire others to select for them. They employ fine-art consultants, or depend on scouts to send them rare textiles from Indonesia or West Africa.

Collecting while abroad is an American tradition started by Thomas Jefferson. Sent to Paris to secure aid for his revolutionary countrymen, he managed also to acquire ideas and treasures for Monticello. A century later, the super-rich "robber barons" bought entire houses of European treasures—including ceilings and walls—to send back to decorate their homes. Less wealthy U.S. travelers bought less, but they still shopped.

Today some of those purchases, along with many things that were brought in by import merchants, are still here, retained by the descendants or other heirs of the rich, donated to museums or in markets of every stratum.

You don't have to be rich to be a collector; you have to have a thirst for acquisition. In addition to the adages of condition and rarity, every appraiser and high-end auctioneer I spoke with emphasized over and over: "Buy what you like, and go from there." The best direction in which to head is toward greater knowledge of your collection field. You want to be prepared to identify and seize a treasure you happen on at a bargain price.

On the other hand, the people most likely to be hurt by a changing market are those of us who suffer from *I-must-have-it-now* syndrome. An autographed Seinfeld script from the 1992-93 season sold at Christies for $22,000 in the hot days of the show. It is now worth only $1,500. The same will happen to souvenirs of "Grey's Anatomy" or "The Sopranos," if it hasn't already. "Avoid buying trends," says Pete Seigel, owner of the gallery, Gotta Have It, in Manhattan.

One *sticky* trend, a trend with seeming staying power, is collecting objects once owned by a celebrity, whether a rock star, a movie star or an ex-president. At a Sotheby's auction in 1996, the high bidder paid $1.43 million for the desk on which John F. Kennedy signed the Nuclear Test Ban Treaty. At the same auction, objects of no historical or even intrinsic value went for staggering amounts of money just because they once belonged to Jackie Kennedy Onassis.

That auction soon became known as the "garage sale of the century" because pillows sold for tens of thousands of dollars, evidence, if any was needed, that Jackie Kennedy had ascended to a position higher than any pop icon. The desire to retain some piece of her "is an effort to stop time in its tracks and makes us feel less stricken," claims Muensterberger. Will the pillows retain their value? Who knows? This may not matter to the satisfied buyer, who can rest her head on the same downy spot where a legendary face once nestled.

In 2006, a dress designed by Givenchy for Audrey Hepburn's "possible use" in the 1961 hit *Breakfast at Tiffany's* sold at a London auction for $800,000, about seven times the reserve price.

We mortals are not competing in most of these bidding wars, but we might take them as warning that when trends rise to high altitude it may be wise to stand back and wait for the stardust to settle.

Public attitudes about all kinds of things affect what we desire. "There is a big return to Americana since 9/11," says the appraiser and popular-culture historian Elyse Luray, who thinks this makes collecting sense. "Our country is much younger than Britain so we only have two hundred and thirty years of history to collect from—1776 to the present," she reminds us. Some Americana is relatively rare. Luray suggests buying American historical documents, American Indian blankets, and anything to do with cowboys. She says, "Even designer items sold today at Target could be the future collectibles. Architect Michael Graves' stainless steel teakettle with a rooster spout sells for $25. Buy it. Keep it in its original box and wait."

There is no limit as to what can be collected. "In fifteen years, you will probably see someone selling a collection of every color iMac computer. There is next to nothing that hasn't been collected—the trick might be to put stuff away for a decade or more, and it will become wildly valuable," says Noel Barrett, an "Antiques Roadshow" appraiser and owner of Noel Barrett Antiques & Auctions, Ltd.

Happy Hunting!

—Linda Abrams

Notable Antique & Collectible Fairs

Although you may have plenty of local antique shopping near your home, sometimes you have to travel to build your collection. Don't let geography stand in your way. Remember some collectibles can be better bought and sold in certain regions of the country. You will find more expensive Civil War items in the south than in the north. Gold rush memorabilia can be found easier in Oregon or northern California than in Texas.

Large antique shows often display vast selections of regional collectibles. Touring and one-stop shopping are fun. For many collectors, heaven consists of acres of ground covered with hundreds, sometimes thousands of exhibitors who come from all over the United States and Canada and, at some shows, Europe and Asia as well. At your footsteps (actually, much walking is involved) will be a huge variety of both high-quality and not-so-great items. Check the schedules for each show before planning your trip, and take this advice from seasoned antique hunters.

Make a list of what you are looking for

It's easy to get distracted with so much to choose from. Decide how much you're willing to spend. Do a quick price-check on the Internet to see the price tags on, and, if possible, selling prices of items you seek. Bring cash, credit cards and your checkbook. Different dealers accept different forms of payment. Paying in cash often gives you a discount or a tax break and speeds up the transaction.

Be prepared

Wear a backpack; take a large canvas bag, or a rolling cart to carry your purchases. If you're buying furniture, bring a large vehicle that will enable you to trans-

port the stuff. Have moving blankets (or towels for small fragile items), rope, scissors and duct tape.

Have a back-up communication system to reach a traveling companion should there be no cell service or if your phone runs out of juice.

Some pros advise making up a T-shirt to wear that says "I COLLECT (whatever it is), so dealers can find you.

Dress for success: Wear comfortable shoes, carry bottled water and snacks. These shows have conces-

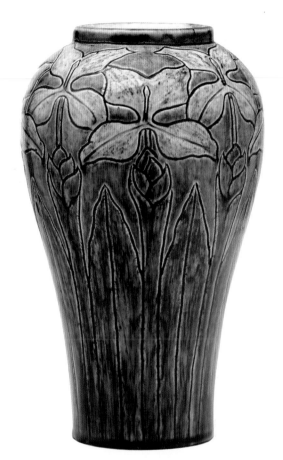

sion stands, but lines could be long.

Arrive early, very early: The best items are snatched up quickly. I have a friend who arrives in the dark with a flashlight so she can be at the starting gate when it opens. Find out if the event offers a preview party. You will pay to get in, but you'll see the best material. If you hate rising early, remember that you can often get bargains near the end of the show from dealers who don't want to drag merchandise home.

Always try to bargain and most especially if an item is flawed. All a dealer can say is, "No."

Notable shows

Brimfield Antiques Show, Brimfield, Massachusetts, held three times a year: May, July, September. This is the largest and most diversified outdoor show in the country.
www.brimfieldshow.com

Atlantique City, Atlantic City, New Jersey, held twice a year, in March and October. This is the largest indoor show in the country.
www.atlantiquecity.com

Antique Week in New England: In one August week, six major shows take place, including ones in Manchester, New Hampshire, and nearby Bedford and more rural Deerfield. For a free show brochure and information, call 603-585-9199.
www.nhada.org/show

Rose Bowl Flea Markets, Pasadena, California. These are held the second Sunday of every month, rain or shine.
www.rgcshows.com

Gold Rush Antique Show & Flea Market in Rochester, Minnesota, held May, August, September. Downtown Oronoco

Gold Rush Days, held in August in Oronoco, Minnesota.
www.goldrushmn.com

Ann Arbor Antiques Market, Ann Arbor, Michigan held on Saturday and Sunday from April through November.
www.annarborantiquesmarket.com

Roundtop, Roundtop, Texas, held twice a year the first weekend in April and October.
www.antiquesweekend.com

Portland Expo Shows, Portland, Oregon, held in March, July and October.
www.palmerwirfs.com
—L.A.

Better Buying Through Reading

Multi-Topic Guides

Kovels' Antiques & Collectibles, by Ralph and Terry Kovel (Black Dog & Leventhal)

Miller's Collectibles Price Guide, edited by Jonty Hearnden and Katherine Higgins (Mitchell Beazley MITCH)

Old West Antiques & Collectibles (Great American Publishing Co.)

The Complete Guide to 20th Century Antiques, by Martin Miller (Carlton Books)

Wade Whimsical Collectibles (Charlton Standard Catalogue), by Pat Murray (The Charlton Press)

Antique Trader: America's Weekly Antiques and Collectibles Marketplace, a weekly periodical and e-newsletter distributed nationally (Krause Publications LTD) www.antiquetrader.com

Furniture & Home Accessories

Sourcebook of Modern Furniture, Third Edition, by Jerryll Habegger and Joseph H. Osman (W. W. Norton)

CARL WARREN

Antique Trader Clocks Price Guide: Including All Types of Clocks 17th Through 20th Century, edited by Kyle Husfloen and Mark Moran (KP Books)

The Encyclopedia of American Art Tiles, 4 volumes by Norman Karlson (Schiffer Publishing)

Warman's Roseville Pottery: Identification and Price Guide by Denise Rago (Krause Publications)

Collecting Head Vases: Identification and Value Guide, by Dave Barron (Collector Books)

Head Vases, by Kathleen Cole (Collector Books)

Wendell August Forge: Seventy Five Years of Artistry in Metal, by Bonita Campbell (Dragonfly Press)

Chasing Rainbows: Collecting American Indian Trade & Camp Blankets, by Barry Friedman, James L. Collins, and Gary Diamond (Bulfinch Press)

Language of the Robe, by Robert W. Kapoun (Gibbs Smith)

Warman's Tools Field Guide, by Clarence Blanchard (Krause Publications)

The ABC's of ABC Ware, by Davida and Irving Shipkowitz (Schiffer Publishing)

The Best of Collectible Dinnerware, by Jo Cunningham (Schiffer Publishing)

Personal Adornments

The Little Book of Mexican Silver Trade and Hallmarks, by Bille Hougart (Tbr International)

Mexican Silver: Modern Handwrought Jewelry & Metalwork, by Penny C. Morrill and Carole A. Berk (Schiffer Publishing)

One Hundred Years of Collectable Jewellery, 1850-1950: An Identification and Value Guide, by Lillian Baker (Collector Books)

Match Holders: 100 Years of Ingenuity, by Denis B. Alsford (Schiffer Publishing)

Pocket Matchsafes: Reflections of Life and Art, 1840-1920, by

W. Eugene Sanders and Christine C. Sanders (Schiffer Publishing)

Bits and Spur Makers in the Texas Tradition: A Historical Perspective, by Ned Martin (Hawk Hill Press)

Gambling Paraphernalia

Gambling Collectible: A Sure Winner, by Leonard Schneir (Schiffer Publishing)

The Hochman Encyclopedia of American Playing Cards, Tom and Judy Dawson (U.S. Game Systems)

STEVE FORTE

Assorted Collectibles

Animation Art Buyer's Guide and Price Guide, by John Cawley

Animation Art: The Early Years 1911-1953, by Jeff Lotman (Schiffer Publishing)

Art Nouveau Postcards, by Rizzoli (Rizzoli)

Book of Penny Toys, by David Pressland (P E I International)

Collection, Use and Care of Historical Photographs, by

ALL PHOTOS COOURTESY OF SWAN AUCTION GALLERY

161

Robert A. Weinstein and Larry Booth (American Association for State and Local History)

Hanna-Barbera Cartoons, by Michael Mallory (Universe)

Wake Up America: World War I and the American Poster, by Walton Rawls (Abbeville Press, 2001)

World War I Posters, by Gary Borkan (Schiffer Publishing, 2002)

Antique Toy World, a monthly periodical (Dale Kelley, Publisher) www.antiquetoyworld.com

—L.A. and M.H.

Glossaries

Auction Room Glossary

Absentee bid: Leaving a bid with the auction house so that it can bid on your behalf.

Auctioneer: The person sitting on the rostrum wielding the gavel and monitoring the bids.

Auction fever: The situation that occurs when a bidder forgets the true value of a lot and bids like a headless chicken.

Auction preview: The days that are allocated for prospective buyers to view all of the items and lots in the saleroom.

Bidders: The people in the saleroom who are attempting to buy goods.

Bidding off the wall: A term used for a shady auctioneer who is taking bids from the wall to get up to a reserve price.

Buyer's premium: The percentage-sum that is added to the hammer price and paid to the auction house.

Cashier: The person who has the pleasure of taking your money when you have bid successfully on a lot..

Catalogue: The publication available from the auctioneer on viewing days and sale days. It contains a complete list of all items entered into the auction.

Commission bid: A bid that is written on a form supplied by the auction house so that it can execute the bid for you.

Condition report: A detailed description of the state of a lot. It can be obtained from the auctioneers via email, phone, post or in person.

Dealers: These are the professional antiques traders that you often see huddled together in an auction room.

Defaulting on a bid: When you do not fulfill a bid. This can be very costly, as the auction house can pursue a claim against you if you do not pay for and collect the lot you bid on in the auction.

Estimates: These figures are provided as a guide to prospective buyers, and are normally based around a reserve price (see opposite).

Hammer price: The final price you pay when the auctioneer's hammer drops.

Invoice: This will list each lot you have purchased, how much you paid for each lot and the total amount you have spent, with the buyer's premium added.

Lot number: The number given to each item coming up for auction.

Paddle number: The specific number that is allocated to each buyer after registration (see below).

Porters: These are the happy faces that walk around the saleroom and point out the lots as they are coming under the hammer. They will also help you pack and move your goods at the end of the sale.

Registering to bid: This is normally done in the head cashier's office. You register with your name, address and some form of identification. Once this is completed you will be given a paddle number with which to bid in the auction.

Reserve Price: The minimum price set by the owner for selling the item.

Selling rate: The number of lots the auctioneer normally sells per hour. This is usually between 80 and 300 lots.

Storage charges: The charge you have to pay if you are late in clearing your items from the saleroom.

Telephone bid: A pre-arranged telephone link that is booked with the auctioneer for the lots you would like to bid on. This method allows bidders to remain anonymous.

Terms of business: The legal jargon that is normally displayed at the back of the saleroom or in the catalogue.

Terms of payment: Most auction houses accept checks, cash and all major credit cards.

Withdrawn lots: Items taken out of a sale by an auction house.

Clock Glossary

Automation: Figures that move or strike on the hour and the quarter-hour.

Balance wheel: The mechanism that controls the movement of a watch or a clock.

Bezel: The ring that secures the glass cover to the dial on a watch or a clock.

Calendar aperture: The small window on some dials that displays the day of the month, and sometimes the month as well.

Chapter ring: The part of the dial on which the hour numbers are painted, engraved or attached.

Escapement: The part of the clock that regulates it and provides the impulse to the chain, pendulum or balance.

Hood: The part of a long-case clock that lifts off the top to provide access to the movement.

Pendulum: The device that swings at a fixed rate and controls the timekeeping.

Repeat button: A small device that lets the clock repeat the last hour or quarter of an hour when a cord is pulled or a button is pressed.

Furniture Glossary

Apron: The decorative shaped skirt of wood that runs under the drawers and between the legs of a table or feet of a chest.

Baluster: A symmetrically-placed shaped turning or slender pillar supporting a railing, a furniture leg.

Banding: Decorative veneer around the edges of some tables, drawers and other items of furniture.

Barley twist: A spiral shape normally favored for turned legs during the second half of the 19th century. The pattern is still in use today.

Bergère: A French term that is applied to chairs with caned backs and seats.

Boulle work: A French form of marquetry using brass and tortoiseshell.

Bowfront: An outwardly curved front that is found mainly on a chest of drawers, or sideboards.

Breakfront: A term normally used for a piece of furniture with a protruding center section.

Brush-in slide: The pull-out slide found on the top of a chest of drawers, normally associated with 18th-century bachelors' chests.

Bun foot: A flattened version of a ball foot that was very popular in Victorian times.

Bureau: A writing desk with a tall front that normally encloses a fitted interior; many also have drawers below.

Cabriole leg: A curving S-shaped leg used on tables and chairs that is synonymous with the 18th century.

Canterbury: A small container used for sheet music or papers.

Chesterfield: A deep-buttoned upholstered settee with no wood showing.

Cheval mirror: A tall, freestanding dressing mirror that is supported by two uprights.

Chinoiserie: Oriental-style decoration or a lacquered pattern applied to furniture.

Claw and ball foot: A support modeled as a ball gripped by a claw.

Commode: A highly decorated chest of drawers or cabinet that is also called 'bombe shaped.''

Console table: A table that stands against a wall, normally

between windows. They sometimes have matching mirrors above and can come in pairs.

Corner chair: A chair with backed splats on two sides that is intended to stand in the corner of a room.

Davenport: A small, compact writing unit that has a sloped top for writing; a large sofa.

Drop-in seat: An upholstered seat frame that sits in the main framework of a chair.

Drop leaf: A table with a fixed central section and hinged sides.

Figuring: The natural grain of wood seen in veneer.

Finial: A decorative turned knob normally applied to the top of bookcases and bureaus.

Frieze: The framework immediately below a tabletop.

Harlequin: A term used to describe a set of chairs that are similar but do not match.

Inlay: Normally brass, mother-of-pearl or veneer, these are set into the surface of a solid piece of furniture or wood.

Ladder-back: A chair with a series of horizontal back rails.

Lion's paw feet: A foot carved as a lion's paw; this style was very popular in the 18th century, but also found on brass castors from the early 19th century.

Marquetry: A highly decorative form of inlay using numerous veneers.

Ormolu: A mount or article that is gilded or gold-colored.

Over-mantle mirror: A mirror designed to hang over a mantle-piece.

Papier maché: Pulped paper that is molded to make small trays or small items of furniture.

Parquetry: A geometrical pattern made from small pieces of veneer.

Patina: The build-up of wax and dirt that gives old furniture its unique look.

Pedestal desk: A flat desk, usually with a leather top, that stands on two flights of drawers.

Pembroke table: A small side table with two small flaps.

Piecrust top: The carved or molded decoration to the edge of a table.

Pole screen: An adjustable fire screen.

Runners: The strips of wood on which drawers slide in and out.

Side table: Any table designed to stand against the wall.

Sofa table: Normally an oblong table with two small, hinged flaps at the ends, that's designed to stand directly behind a sofa.

Stretchers: The horizontal bars that strengthen chairs.

Toilet mirror: A small dressing mirror with a drawer below.

Trefoil: Any item that resembles a clover leaf.

Whatnot: A small stand with open display shelves.

Wheel-backed chair: A chair with a circular back and spoke-like support.

Pottery and Porcelain Glossary

Applied decoration: Anything that is attached to a piece rather than being a part of the main body.

Baluster vase: A vase with a curved shape and a narrow stem or neck.

Basalt: A black volcanic stoneware, used frequently by Wedgwood.

Blue and white: A general term used for porcelain and earthenware that has a Chinese-style decoration.

Blanc de Chine: A very translucent type of Chinese porcelain that is still being produced today. It is left unpainted and has a thick glaze.

Bone china: A term commonly used for English porcelain.

Cabinet ware: Plates, cups and saucers made for display rather than for everyday use. These pieces are normally hand-painted and of good quality.

Cancellation mark: One or two strokes through the factory mark that let the buyer know that the item is flawed and not of their normal standard.

Cartouche: A decorative oval frame that is set within the porcelain and normally hand-painted or printed.

Celadon: A term used for the green glaze that is often used on Chinese and Korean stoneware.

Coffee can: A straight-sided cylindrical cup with no handles in a style made famous by Sevres.

Commemorative ware: Any item that commemorates an event, such as a wedding, jubilee or battle.

Crackleware: A form of decoration used on an item, normally Chinese.

Crazing: Tiny surface cracks in the glaze of a piece of porcelain that has been caused by technical defects.

Delft ware: Earthenware made in the Netherlands with a tin glaze (see opposite).

Enamels: The bright colors applied to pottery and porcelain as over-glazed decoration.

Faïence ware: Tin-glazed earthenware that originated in France, Germany and other European countries.

Famille rose or verte: Chinese decoration of either pink (rose) or green (verte) enamel.

Firing crack: Damage to a piece of pottery that has occurred during firing.

Flambé: A bright crimson glaze.

Flat back: A term used for a ceramic figure that has a plain, flat back so that it stands easily on a fireplace mantle.

Gilding: A term used for the application of gold, normally to the banding of porcelain made in the Chinese manner.

Impressed mark: A mark that is indented into the piece by the factory makers.

Incised mark: A mark that is scratched into the surface.

Ironstone china: A type of English stoneware.

Jardinière: A plant or flower container, these are sometimes formed of two pieces with a matching stand.

Lead-glazed: A type of transparent glaze that incorporated lead oxide.

Loving cup: A twin-handled cup that is normally urn-shaped.

Mustache cup: A cup that is specially designed so that its lower lip protects the user from being left with a soiled mustache.

Over-glazed: This is decoration painted or printed on the piece of pottery or porcelain after glazing.

Parian ware: Un-glazed biscuit porcelain similar to Parian marble.

It was popular in the 19th century for figures and figurines.

Pearl ware: A very durable form of white porcelain that was particularly popular at Wedgwood.

Porcelain: A translucent white ceramic that is very fragile.

Pottery: A generic term for all ceramics, excluding porcelain.

Puzzle jug: An unusual jug with a globular body and three or seven spouts at the rim.

Rococo: A popular style of mid-18th-century decoration, which is normally asymmetric and with the use of scrolls.

Soft-paste porcelain: Another term for porcelain that is made in a particular way.

Studio pottery: Pottery that has been individually designed and crafted.

Tea bowl: A small cup inspired by the Asian fashion for tea. These bowls have no handles and were mass-produced.

Terracotta: Lightly fired red earthenware that is not usually glazed.

Tin glaze: An opaque white glaze containing tin, popular in the 18th and 19th centuries and often used on majolica.

Transfer print: A form of decoration which uses a printed engraving.

Silver Glossary

Assay mark: A date-stamp given to silver produced in Britain, Ireland and Scotland that indicates that the silver has been properly tested and is pure.

Beading: A decorative border of small beads around an item of silver.

Bezel: The inner rim of a cover, it is normally used in descriptions of coffee pots and teapots.

British plate: An early version of silver-plating that dates from the 1830s-1850s, and was thereafter called electroplating.

Cartouche: A decorative frame or panel that normally surrounds a coat of arms.

Chalice: Another name for a goblet or wine cup of the type often used at Catholic or Episcopal services.

Charger: A large round under-plate.

Chasing: Decoration that is worked into a silver item with a hammer or a punch. This sort of pattern is raised above the surface.

Cruet: The framework for bottles containing condiments, such as salt, pepper, oil or vinegar.

Dish ring: An unusual item of silver normally used as a trivet. These pieces usually have concave sides, pierced work and come in animal shapes. Most are Irish.

Electroplating: Silver applied over a copper or nickel alloy, a style that was in use from about 1840.

Ewer: A large jug with a lip, which is often part of a set with a basin. It is sometimes used to contain water so that diners can wash their hands during meals.

Filigree: Open decorative panels with small beads. Today's filigree normally comes from Spain, India or Africa.

Flatware: Technically this is a term for all flat objects such as plates and silver, but more recently it has been applied to services of spoons and forks.

Floating or erasure: To remove an existing coat of arms and replace it with another.

Gardroning: A border around the edge of an item, usually formed from a succession of leaves and flutes.

Gilding: A method of applying a gold finish to silver or electro-plated items.

Right cut: A common form of engraving that makes the design work stand out more sharply.

Salver: A flat dish which is similar to a serving tray, but has no handles.

Sterling silver: A term for silver that contains at least 92.5 percent pure silver.

—M.H.

A rare match
Made in Lon
by the

Acknowledgements

I would like to acknowledge my best friend and wife Lesley for all her help in typing my books. Thanks also to the Victoria and Albert Museum in London for having an endless reference library to inspire me; DMG Antiques fairs, and Newark and Ardingly for allowing me and my excellent photographer, Carl Warren to take the shots; my very excellent buddy Mr. David Dickinson who changed the face of the antique television show in England, for his help and support since our meeting in 2000. Finally, my appreciation to New Holland for their superb support while writing.

—M.H.

I offer thanks to my daughter Lisa for her patience and computer assistance; Patty Kranis, manager of Ole Carousel Antiques Center in the Hudson Valley, for feeding my weekend antiquing addictions, Christies auctioneer and PBS host Elyse Luray for sharing her vast knowledge of popular arts (she sold Judy Garland's ruby slippers in May, 2000 for $666,000); Noel Barrett, a gentleman, antique-toy scholar and dealer; Nick Lowry, president of Swann Gallery in New York, and Teri Rosvald of Copperton Lane, an online collectibles company, who took the time to search for fine nursery-ware while she was moving from Utah to Idaho. My thanks also go to Barry Friedman, the authority on trade blankets, for his wonderful humor, insights and photos; Thomas Deupree, an innovative collector and aficionado of vernacular snapshots; Steve Forte, who houses, perhaps, the largest private collection of gambling memorabilia and tirelessly pointed out their distinctions. My appreciation also goes to dice man Kevin Cook, who provided invaluable detail on his forte, and to knife makers Steve Schwarzer and Dellana. This book would be poorer but for the information provided by Brian Lebel, who sits high in the saddle as an expert in Western collectibles; George Sparacio, president of the International Match Safe Association; Rocio Honigmann for her great taste and photos of Taxco Jewelry; Scott Wells, for his overview of American Art tiles; Robert Pearlman and Gary Piattoni for their expertise in space memorabilia; Stephen Holder for allowing me access to his fine collection of Art Nouveau and Art Deco postcards; Bonnie Wood for her enthusiasm about and photos of lady head vases; Art Goldman, who could write his own book on animation cels; and New York gallery owner Pete Siegel.

—L.A.

CARL WARREN

Index